Kevin McCruden's introduction to the four Gospels and letters of Paul combines a thorough familiarity with serious scholarship and a sensitivity to the important questions that new readers bring to these ancient texts. Within a framework defined by religious experience and the common life and with a view to their impact on modern interpreters, McCruden offers a sensitive reading rich in insight. His work is a superb tool for introducing undergraduates to the critical study of the New Testament.

—Harry Attridge
Yale Divinity School

Professors of New Testament as well as leaders of Bible study groups often find themselves searching for outside sources in the biblical field that go beyond the strictly academic analysis of the New Testament texts to address the personal experience of the community members and how that holds coherence with our current reality.

It is precisely for this reason that Kevin McCruden's *On the Way* distinguishes itself from other scholarly introductions to the Gospels and the letters of Paul. Without any mitigation of the scholarly knowledge necessary for the understanding of each document, and with his gift for gracefully communicating erudition in a smooth readable style, McCruden trains his special focus on those most pertinent texts that evince the convert's personal life and his or her desire to commit to community, and then moves to discussions of contemporary heroes and issues of religio-socio-political recent history.

As a result, McCruden effectively connects the Gospels and letters of Paul to our own world, as vibrant conversation partners from across the millennia, where we find common ground in their evidence of personal transformation and a community commitment that becomes a passion and joy.

—Wendy Cotter, CSJ
Loyola University Chicago

Kevin McCruden has convincingly traced the thread that runs through a significant portion of the canonical New Testament, the four Gospels, and the undisputed letters of Paul. Each of these books originated in the lived experience of the communal encounter of the Risen Christ, shared by its author and immediate audience.

By identifying the power of the shared religious experience of the communities of the New Testament in all its diversity, McCruden has opened a horizon for contemporary readers to understand more deeply their own encounter with the same Christ. A wide audience that includes students, teachers, and pastors will benefit from his insightful, focused, and lucid reading of the Gospels and Paul.

—Alan C. Mitchell
Georgetown University

In *On the Way*, McCruden consistently offers insightful interpretations of the relationship between the religious experience of God and living life in community as this relationship is reflected in the four Gospels and the letters of Paul. He writes in an enviably clear and delightful style. The reader not only learns a great deal but does so with pleasure. McCruden has a knack for clarifying without oversimplifying.

—Thomas H. Tobin, SJ
Loyola University Chicago

ON

Religious Experience and Common Life

THE

in the Gospels and Letters of Paul

WAY

KEVIN B. McCRUDEN

ANSELM
ACADEMIC

Created by the publishing team of Anselm Academic.

The scriptural quotations contained herein are from the New Revised Standard Version of the Bible (unless otherwise noted). Copyright © 1993 and 1989 by the Division of Christian Education of the National Council of the Churches of Christ in the United States of America. All rights reserved.

Cover image: A fourth century fresco representing the raising of Lazarus from the Via Latina Catacomb, Rome. © Scala / Art Resource, NY

Printed in the United States of America

7093

ISBN 978-1-59982-793-3

Dedication

For Kerry, Liam, and Samuel

∽

Author Acknowledgments

I express my deep gratitude and thanks to the many friends and colleagues who have helped support this project along the way either by offering encouragement or helpful critique. Amy Jill-Levine patiently read through early versions of the first four chapters of the manuscript and provided incisive feedback on the material relating to the Synoptic Gospels. Harry Attridge, Tom Tobin, along with several of my colleagues at Gonzaga, in particular Megan McCabe and Shannon Dunn, all read through earlier versions of portions of the manuscript and offered thoughtful feedback especially regarding issues of voice and tone. I owe an especially overwhelming debt of gratitude to the publishing and editorial staff at Anselm Academic. Paul Peterson's detailed editorial work as well as insightful comments have made this book much clearer and more persuasive than I could have accomplished on my own. And I cannot say enough good things about Maura Hagarty, who was the first to see a potential value in the project and whose commitment to the project never wavered. Throughout the writing of this book I have endeavored to keep foremost in my mind the mission of Anselm Academic to provide books that are both engaging and useful to undergraduates. My hope is that I have succeeded in this goal, if only in a modest way.

Publisher Acknowledgments

Thank you to the following individuals who reviewed this work in progress:

Sherri Brown, *Creighton University, Omaha, Nebraska*

Timothy Milinovich, *Dominican University, River Forest, Illinois*

Then they came to Capernaum; and when he was in the house he asked them, "What were you arguing about on the way?" But they were silent, for on the way they had argued with one another who was the greatest.

—Mark 9:33-34

Contents

Preface for Teachers

Recently a colleague appeared at my office door wondering aloud whether students today find courses on scripture too remote from their lived experience. At that instant I could not help but recall an especially honest and humorous course evaluation I received some time ago in which a student praised my ability to "make an inherently uninteresting topic like the New Testament somewhat interesting." Needless to say, I could immediately relate to my colleague's sentiment. At the same time, I also sensed something else behind my colleague's apprehension, namely, the recognition of how demanding the vocation of teaching can be for those who care deeply about the craft and desire to reach students where they are.

Whether as a result of cultural forces, institutional priorities, some combination of these, or perhaps other factors altogether, the task of introducing undergraduates to the academic study of scripture—in my own case the writings of the New Testament—does appear to be becoming ever more challenging. It is true that there are certain perennial challenges that go with the territory. Students always struggle, for example, to engage empathetically with texts that take as given the existence of a tripartite cosmos, or that espouse the belief that all of history will soon come to an end. These particular pedagogical speedbumps are, however, the relatively easy ones to navigate. Shaped by such contemporary cultural events as the me-too movement, the black lives matter movement, the migrant crisis at the border, and the clergy sexual abuse scandal, an ever growing number of students find deeply challenging—as they should—writings that raise problematic concerns relating to complex issues associated with ethnicity, gender, and class dynamics. Much of my work in the classroom focuses increasingly on guiding students in their articulation of these issues, reflecting with students on the relationship of these issues to the scriptural text, and encouraging students to discover ways in which the writings of the New Testament might offer resources for wrestling with the complexity of issues that impinge upon their lives. When I am successful in this work many of my students arrive at the end of the semester less convinced in their judgment that the writings of the New Testament really are as remote from their experience as they may have thought upon entering the course.

This book explores the relevance of the study of the New Testament for lived experience by analyzing the topics of religious experience and common life as these are revealed in the New Testament Gospels and letters of Paul. The essential point of the study is that these writings function, at their most fundamental level, to articulate powerful experiences of personal encounter that result in the commitment to embody new patterns of living within community. This claim is, at the same time, quite problematic for the simple reason that the attempt to define what religious experience actually refers to is complicated by the fact that all human experiences are interpreted experiences. That is, human creativity always plays an essential role not only in the shaping, but also in the generation of any experience that is invested with ultimate meaning. The same dynamic is also evident in connection with the new patterns of behavior or common life that have as their purpose the translation of religious experience into action. Both on the individual and on the communal level, the embodying of religious experience in concrete behavior inevitably entails human creativity in the quest to discover meaning and ultimacy in our lives.

In this study I do not claim to give any sort of definitive treatment to the themes of religious experience and common life. Similarly, I must admit that I have been selective in the specific content drawn from the Gospels and letters of Paul that I have singled out for analysis. While the material I have chosen does reflect my judgment about what is particularly illustrative of the themes of religious experience and common life, this choice of material is by no means exhaustive. Students who read this book and immerse themselves in deep reading of the Gospels and letters of Paul will likely make connections that I have missed.

Religious Experience and the Common Life

My favorite novel is the nineteenth-century masterpiece by Victor Hugo, *Les Misérables*. While there are many parts of the story that I enjoy, I am impressed most by Hugo's gift for illuminating timely issues of social justice through his sketching of such memorable characters as Jean Valjean, Fantine, and the young orphan girl, Cosette. Equally engaging are the many instances in the novel where Hugo explores the religious implications of the experiences of his characters. One of these instances involves the compassionate bishop Monseigneur Bienvenu, who appears at the beginning of *Les Mis*érables as an exemplary religious figure whose depth of piety is complemented by his humility and acts of kindness to others.

> He was indulgent toward women and the poor, upon whom the weight of society falls most heavily. He would say, "The faults of women, children, and servants, and of the weak, the indigent and the ignorant, are the faults of husbands, fathers and masters, of the strong, the rich and the wise. . . ." Clearly, he had his own strange way of judging things. I suspect he acquired it from the Gospels.[1]

Hugo does not specify what episodes from the Gospels have influenced the portrayal of his fictional bishop. It might even be the case

---

1. Victor Hugo, *Les Misérables*, trans. Lee Fahnestock and Norman MacAfee (New York: Signet, 2013), 13–14.

that what Hugo refers to as the "Gospels" has more to do with a pattern of living for others that, according to the Gospels, informed the life and teachings of the historical Jesus of Nazareth.[2] Whatever were Hugo's intentions on this matter, I appreciate how he invites the reader to reflect on the relationship between religious experience and the living out of such experience in ways that challenge self-centered attitudes and behavior. I also find intriguing the suggestion that this relationship has something to do with the capacity of religious experience to transform how persons see and treat other human beings in community, particularly in ways that promote justice and reconciliation in place of selfishness and dominance.

The principal character and hero of *Les Misérables* is Jean Valjean. He first appears in the novel as a paroled convict attempting to return to society only to meet with unkindness and reproach from everyone he encounters. Nineteen years in prison had hardened him against humanity; his fresh exposure to the persistent harshness of society serves even more sharply to constrict his soul. This all changes, however, when Valjean meets the gentle bishop Myriel Bienvenu. Bewildered by the bishop's hospitality and kindness, and inspired by his solemn consecration of Valjean's soul, Jean Valjean begins the painful process of opening his life to the potentiality of transformation and renewal. Much of the remainder of Hugo's novel is given over to the narration of Jean Valjean's journey of learning to love and to live for others, especially the orphan girl, Cosette. As the story unfolds, the reader begins to suspect that a deeper divine pedagogy is at work behind Valjean's choices, sacrificing self-interest for the benefit of others. By the novel's end, this pedagogy transforms a convict into a saint.

Taking inspiration from these characters in Hugo's *Les Misérables*, this study explores the relationship between religious experience and common life as it appears in the writings of the New Testament Gospels and the letters of the Apostle Paul. Given this project, at least three questions present themselves at the outset of this study: (1) How are the concepts of religious experience

---

2. Both Craig R. Koester and Michael J. Gorman employ the term *cruciform*, meaning cross-like, to describe the self-giving of Jesus that led ultimately to his execution. See Craig R. Koester, *Symbolism in the Fourth Gospel: Meaning, Mystery, Community*, 2nd ed. (Minneapolis: Fortress, 2003), 246. See also Michael J. Gorman, *Apostle of the Crucified Lord: A Theological Introduction to Paul and His Letters* (Grand Rapids: Eerdmans, 2002), 118–19.

In the 1978 film adaptation of *Les Misérables*, Bishop Myriel Bienvenu (Claude Dauphin) gives costly silver candlesticks to convict Jean Valjean (Richard Jordan), solemnly charging Valjean to commit the remainder of his life to becoming a righteous man.

and common life to be defined? (2) Why choose these specific texts to serve as the basis for this study when other writings besides the Gospels and the letters of Paul appear in the New Testament? (3) What kinds of interpretive methods and intellectual commitments will guide this study?

What Does Religious Experience Signify?

Luke T. Johnson offers the following proposal for how to think about the diversity of writings that comprise the New Testament: "The NT writings approach us as witnesses to and interpretations of specifically religious claims having to do with the experience of God as mediated through Jesus."[3] This proposal raises what is perhaps the

---

3. Luke Timothy Johnson, *The Writings of the New Testament*, 3rd ed. (Minneapolis: Fortress, 2010), 6. For a more detailed treatment of the topic of religious experience, see Luke Timothy Johnson, *Religious Experience in Earliest Christianity: A Missing Dimension in New Testament Studies* (Minneapolis: Fortress, 1998).

most basic of questions about the origins of the New Testament: Why, in fact, do these texts exist at all? Not surprisingly, no single answer can be given. A variety of factors, inclusive of complex historical, social, and literary dynamics all contributed to the emergence of the twenty-seven writings that comprise the New Testament. Among the many forces that shaped this process, however, Johnson privileges the role that religious experience exercised in the evolution of these texts. But what in fact is signified by the concept of religious experience?

The concept of religious experience—much like the concept of religion itself—is difficult to capture in any simple definition.[4] Even the term *experience* appears to elude any unambiguous definition. In terms of general usage, the category of experience is perhaps used most often to denote a personal reaction to someone or something. That is, an experience is something that makes some sort of impression on a person by engaging the affective, intellectual, and psychological dimensions of human consciousness. But what, then, might the definition of religious experience be? Some see religious experience as having to do with a perception of reality that is considered to be transcendent; that is, a reality understood to be absolute, suprahuman, and otherwordly. Perhaps the most classic example of such a definition of religious experience is to be found in the writings of Mircea Eliade, who describes the religious person as one who "always believes that there is an absolute reality, the sacred, which transcends this world, but manifests itself in this world, thereby sanctifying it and making it real."[5] For Eliade the perception of transcendence comprises the essence of all that qualifies as religious experience; moreover, it is this perception of absolute reality that, according to Eliade, enables human beings to find meaning and orientation in the world.[6] Also integral to Eliade's definition

---

4. Indeed for someone like Jonathan Z. Smith the concept of religion has no reference to any sort of objective reality at all; it functions purely as an academic term created for the purpose of describing and analyzing certain kinds of human activities. See Jonathan Z. Smith, *Imagining Religion: From Babylon to Jonestown*, Chicago Studies in the History of Judaism (Chicago: University of Chicago Press, 1982), xii.

5. Mircea Eliade, *The Sacred and the Profane: The Nature of Religion*, trans. Willard R. Trask (New York: Harcourt, 1959), 202.

6. Eliade, *Sacred and Profane*, 23.

of religious experience is the insistence that absolute reality, or the sacred, manifests itself to human beings, who then find themselves in the position of having to respond to such disclosure. For someone like Eliade, therefore, religious experience ultimately involves the experience of a reality that the human subject encounters as Other than itself.[7]

Other contemporary theorists of religion, however, have offered other proposals for defining religious experience, beginning with the observation that religious experience cannot easily be separated from the role that human creativity exerts in terms of both shaping and generating such experience.[8] The human quest for meaning, as Ann Taves observes, is a quest that is never undertaken in isolation from other modes of connectivity. As particular human persons, we all find ourselves embedded within, and interacting with, a complex web of social, psychological, spiritual, cognitive, and cultural contexts, all of which influence the vast variety of experiences that define our lives.[9] This is true of religious experiences as well.

Religious Experience as a Mode of Encounter

Returning once more to Luke T. Johnson's definition, it is clear that for Johnson religious experience has to do fundamentally with the perception of what can be termed ultimate or transcendent reality. Johnson defines religious experience, then, much as Eliade does, as an encounter with a reality that, on the face of it, seems like a contradiction: an encounter with a reality experienced as wholly Other than oneself, but at the same time an encounter that is experienced as intensely personal, life-changing, and real. It should be noted, however, that Johnson makes a point of specifying that what is perceived as transcendent reality is always a reality perceived by an experiencing subject.[10] What Johnson means is that the nature of any religious experience should be understood as relationally true, and not

---

7. Eliade, *Sacred and Profane*, 11.

8. Ann Taves, *Revelatory Events: Three Case Studies of the Emergence of New Spiritual Paths* (Princeton: Princeton University Press, 2016).

9. See Taves, *Revelatory Events*, 290–95.

10. Johnson, *Religious Experience*, 56–60.

necessarily objectively true.[11] It is impossible, in other words, to do away with the irreducible perspectival nature of such experiences. Whenever this perspectival aspect of religious experience is overlooked there is a danger of falling into discourse that defines specific religious experiences as either unique or universal, and thereby more legitimate than other religious experiences. Despite this danger, Johnson suggests that the category of transcendence is still essential to retain, since only the language of transcendence is able to give adequate expression to those experiences that are perceived—for whatever reason—to break the bounds of our more familiar, day to day categories for explaining the world around us.[12]

The insights of Robert Orsi on this topic might help to clarify the foregoing observations. Orsi notes that the intellectual developments that began in Enlightenment Europe and that gave rise to the modern world have made the very concept of transcendence a less obvious explanatory tool for mapping our awareness today of what counts as truly real.[13] Defining transcendence as meaningful presence, Orsi observes that, "Western modernity exists under the sign of absence. Time and space are emptied of presence."[14] As a result, Orsi argues that modern notions of what constitutes religion are typically interpreted against the background of the more familiar and generally more accepted categories of scientific methods of inquiry. At the same time, Orsi recognizes that experiences of the "the eruption of presence" are not entirely absent from our lives.[15] Individuals and communities still do on occasion speak of experiences in which "the transcendent broke into time."[16] Orsi proposes that linguistic expressions are therefore needed in our contemporary setting that do justice to experiences of meaningful presences that individuals and communities judge to be real, but that push up against the limits of

---

11. Johnson, *Religious Experience*, 61–62.

12. Johnson, *Religious Experience*, 59.

13. Robert A. Orsi, "Abundant History: Marian Apparitions as Alternative Modernity," in *Recent Themes in American Religious History: Historians in Conversation*, ed. Randall J. Stephens (Columbia, SC: University of South Carolina Press, 2009), 127–39.

14. Orsi, "Abundant History," 131.

15. Orsi, "Abundant History," 132.

16. Orsi, "Abundant History," 128.

modern critical theories of explanation. The term Orsi proposes for such experiences is *abundant events*.[17]

By employing this term, Orsi seeks to capture as many of the multiple factors as possible that flow into highly personal religious experiences of transcendence. He points out that these factors are often profoundly relational, encompassing a subject's relationship and interaction with the surrounding culture, family, acquaintances, and social groupings, often over periods of many years. Such relationships, and the emotional and intellectual commitments they engender and nurture, interact in complex ways with experiences of transcendence. They provide both the foundation for such experience as well as the ground for investing the experience with new meanings that in turn bring forth into existence new modes of behavior and interaction with others. With such a rich, scholarly conversation on the definition of religious experience in the background, what might an exploration of the themes of religious experience and common life as disclosed in the writings of the New Testament look like?

Giving Expression to Religious Experience

While the texts that comprise the New Testament do not present anything like a flat, homogenous witness to the person of Jesus of Nazareth, they do share a fundamental religious claim that sounds clearly within all their diversity. This claim is that, through his life, death, and above all resurrection, Jesus both embodies and discloses God's ultimate purposes for the world and is now alive in a new and more powerful way through being raised from the dead. It is crucial to recognize that no part of this claim is open to historical, empirical verification; the claim is inherently perspectival in the sense that it is nurtured by the religious experience that Jesus is a living presence available to those who profess faith in him. One way to think, then, about the writings of the New Testament is to view them as diverse and creative articulations of an experience of an encounter with the divine understood to be mediated through the presence of the risen Jesus. It is important

---

17. Orsi, "Abundant History," 133.

to emphasize that this encounter should be understood as a real encounter; it is real, however, in a relational rather than an objective, empirical sense.[18] That is, what is encountered is perceived to be a personal presence or power recognized as absolute by specific persons within a specific community that shares a common outlook and shared commitments.[19]

The element of personal involvement is always integral to the experience of an encounter with transcendence. The following passage taken from the Gospel of John helps to clarify this observation. Reckoning honestly with the fact that he has not narrated every single event or "sign" of Jesus' ministry that could be included in his narrative, the author of John's Gospel says this about the signs that have been included: "But these are written so that you may come to believe that Jesus is the Messiah, the Son of God, and that through believing you may have life in his name" (John 20:31).[20] In designating Jesus as the "Messiah" and the "Son of God," the author of John's Gospel does not intend to present the reader with anything like a propositional truth claim that can be proven empirically. Rather, the nature of the truth claims that we encounter in the Fourth Gospel—and indeed in all four Gospels—is relational and experiential. That is, they are claims that give expression to deeply personal and communal religious experience. To put this another way, both the author and the intended audience of John's Gospel

---

18. Sandra Schneiders voices a similar idea in her theory of the nature of religious statements: "The affirmation of divine disclosure is, strictly speaking, a faith affirmation. The believer claims to perceive what some others, confronted with the same phenomenon, do not perceive. The most the believer can do is describe and explain the experience. It is useless to try to prove, from the phenomenon itself, *that* it is disclosive of the divine." See Sandra M. Schneiders, *The Revelatory Text: Interpreting the New Testament as Sacred Scripture* (San Francisco: Harper, 1991), 50.

19. See Luke T. Johnson, *Religious Experience*, 184.

20. There is an interesting translation issue involved with the conclusion of chapter 20 of John's Gospel in verse 31. Depending on how one translates the Greek verb for "to believe," the meaning changes somewhat from a summons to come to belief for the first time as opposed to a call for the community to keep believing. In other words, rather than concerned with a missionary campaign to bring persons to faith, the author of the Fourth Gospel is writing to those already committed to a belief in Jesus. The translation presented in the NRSV best captures the underlying Greek preserved in the earliest and best manuscripts of John's Gospel. See Francis J. Moloney, *The Gospel of John*, ed. Daniel J. Harrington, SJ, Sacra Pagina 4 (Collegeville, MN: Liturgical Press, 1998), 544.

encounter the living Jesus in their lives as a figure of ultimate significance, someone who makes possible a life of renewed fellowship both with God and with one another. John's Gospel represents an attempt at articulating, however imperfectly, something of the shape and quality of this experience of encounter.

None of these observations should be taken to suggest that the authors of the Gospels were uninterested in the task of preserving the historical memory of Jesus. The topic of the historical reliability of the Gospels is more complex, however, than it might at first seem. Since the Gospels appear as though they purport to offer a factual, historical narrative, many readers assume that historical objectivity must have been the primary goal of these texts. Modern readers need to understand, however, that when they assume that these writings are meant to be "history," they are expecting the Gospels to conform to a genre of writing that simply did not exist in the ancient world. To be sure, "historical" writings existed, but the ancient genre of history was very different from the modern one. For example, in many instances ancient authors had at best only a general idea of the sort of things said by, say, a specific general addressing his troops before a battle, or a politician advocating before a public assembly a particular political course of action to take, speeches that may have been delivered a hundred years or more before the historian's own day. The author's job was to *compose* a speech that fit the occasion and was in keeping with the point he wished to make.[21] Ancient audiences knew this, and did not expect that the speeches they encountered in a history were necessarily the exact words of the character being depicted. Similarly, a given saying of Jesus recorded in the Gospels may well reflect the collective memory of something that Jesus said, but it is hard to imagine that readers at that time expected the saying to preserve the actual words of Jesus verbatim. Such an expectation was altogether alien to ancient literature; one does well, then, not to impose modern expectations on ancient genres. More will be said below on the issue of historical reliability with regard to the genre of the Gospels as examples of ancient biographies.

---

21. The use of the masculine pronoun here reflects the fact that, as far as we know, all the surviving histories from the ancient world were written by men.

Defining the Concept of Common Life

To an impressive degree, the writings of the New Testament focus less on the individual than on the communal. This is just one of the many ways in which the biblical text challenges the modern post-industrial approach to viewing reality. Contemporary US culture in particular tends to operate on the assumption that a person's identity is the outcome of some combination of unique personal gifts interacting with the personal choices that one makes. On an intellectual level Americans may be aware of being born into various kinds of collectives, such as a particular family and culture, but they typically act in ways that imply that identity is understood largely in individualistic ways. For example, enormous significance is placed on values such as personal responsibility, individual rights, and self-actualization. As one might expect, these values inevitably shape for both good and ill not only one's sense of self, but also one's interpersonal behavior.

In contrast to this accustomed individualism, an inclination toward the communal characterized the sensibilities of the authors responsible for the creation of the writings found in the New Testament. For example, one of the first episodes readers encounter at the beginning of the public ministry of Jesus as described in the four Gospels is a scene where Jesus summons his first followers (Matt. 4:18–22; Mark 1:16–20; Luke 5:1–11; John 1:35–51). While the details of the episode differ from Gospel to Gospel, all four accounts agree that Jesus was highly intentional about sharing his mission and message with others. From the very beginning, the small cells of believers who responded to the message of the Gospel also sought to actualize that message in a communal setting.

This emphasis on the theme of community also characterizes the letters of Paul and is seen, for example, in Paul's use of the metaphor of the "body" (Rom. 12:4–5; 1 Cor. 12:12–27). By visualizing the community as the body of Christ, Paul reflects on how the presence of the risen Jesus is made powerfully tangible and real only when every member of the community is honored, especially the vulnerable and less socially powerful members of the group. Integral to the persuasive power of the body metaphor is the communal implication that without the diversity of many kinds of people there

The Metropolitan Museum of Art, Johnston Fund, 1924

Jesus summons Simon Peter and his brother Andrew in this sixth-century Byzantine mosaic representing Luke 5:1-11. All four Gospels agree that one of Jesus' first acts was to assemble a community of followers.

can be no community at all; indeed, the risen Jesus is encountered, according to Paul, precisely within the diverse lives and faces of all who make up the community. This example taken from Paul points to an important dimension of the definition of common life that will be developed in this study. Integral to the religious experience of encounter with God through the presence of the risen Jesus is the accompanying commitment to embody such experience in and through behavior that witnesses to transformation.

Why the Gospels and Why the Letters of Paul?

The decision to focus upon the New Testament Gospels and the correspondence of Paul is informed both by historical and religious considerations. Although a number of writings similar to the Gospels existed in the early church, the four canonical Gospels are the earliest narratives committed to articulating the shape of the human career of Jesus and the early Christian belief in his resurrection from the dead. While the precise process by which these accounts attained an authoritative status remains obscure, the wide appeal of these four narratives to geographically diverse audiences suggests that the basic story they tell resonated with many early Christians as normative in some way.[22] That is, already by the mid-second century CE there appears to have been a consensus that these writings best captured what a plurality of early Christians wished to say about Jesus as they reflected on their shared experience of the religious significance of the life, death, and resurrection of Jesus of Nazareth.

The attentive reader will observe the text using the term *Christian* to refer to both the belief system and social makeup of the audiences for the Gospels. This term can be misleading, however, since it might suggest to readers the image of self-identified members of a specific religion called Christianity. In fact, nothing like a separate religion called Christianity existed in the historical period in which the writings of the New Testament took shape. During this formative period the community that would become Christianity existed as a sect within Judaism, the religious tradition from which it emerged. Nonetheless, throughout this study we will use the terms *Christian* and *Christianity* as customary designations for this sect and movement within ancient Judaism.

Estimated Dates of Composition

Undisputed letters of Paul	50-60 CE
Gospel of Mark	69-70 CE
Gospel of Matthew	80-95 CE
Gospel of Luke	80-95 CE
Gospel of John	90-95 CE

---

22. For all of their distinctiveness the four Gospels share in common an intense focus on the events of the suffering and death of Jesus. See Luke Timothy Johnson, *The Real Jesus: The Misguided Quest for the Historical Jesus and the Truth of the Traditional Gospels* (San Francisco: Harper, 1996), 141–66.

Written even earlier than the canonical Gospels, the undisputed letters of Paul provide another window into early Christian thinking about the significance of the life, death, and resurrection of Jesus. Scholars employ the term *undisputed* in order to make a distinction between letters most likely written by Paul and those that may have been written by later followers of Paul. Altogether there are thirteen letters attributed to Paul in the New Testament. Based largely on an analysis of perceived stylistic and thematic affinities, seven of these letters (Romans, 1 and 2 Corinthians, Galatians, Philippians, 1 Thessalonians, and Philemon) are acknowledged by most scholars as genuinely authored by Paul. The six remaining letters attributed to Paul (Ephesians, Colossians, 2 Thessalonians, 1 and 2 Timothy, and Titus) are typically designated under the category of "disputed" or "contested," meaning that their authorship by Paul is considered by many scholars to be either uncertain or that something more complex than simple authorship was involved in their composition, such as collaboration or delegation by Paul.[23]

Apart from a brief notice in the Gospel of Luke to an otherwise unknown patron by the name of Theophilus, the Gospel narratives do not identify their intended audiences. By contrast, Paul's letters provide a much clearer glimpse of the ancient communities that gathered in response to the early Christian proclamation about Jesus. We see this heightened communal character in Paul's customary manner of designating his addressees as "assemblies" (see Gal. 1:2). In the ancient Mediterranean world, "assembly," or in Greek *ekklēsia*,[24] referred to a civic body constituted by citizens of a region; the basic meaning of the word, therefore, was that of an assembled community. Quite fittingly, then, Paul's purpose in writing letters to the local communities that he called "assemblies" or "churches" had a clear communal function, namely, to support early Christians as they attempted to integrate their religious convictions about Jesus into patterns of behavior that complemented their beliefs.

For this reason, the subject matter and themes of Paul's letters appear quite different from the subject matter and themes found in the New Testament Gospels. While Paul is certainly aware of the

---

23. See Maria Pascuzzi, *Paul: Windows on His Thought and World* (Winona, MN: Anselm Academic, 2014), 20–21.

24. In subsequent centuries, *ekklēsia* would come to mean "church."

major events of Jesus' career, nowhere in his letters does Paul purport to give an extended account of the life and death of Jesus as do the Gospels. Instead, Paul's interest is oriented toward the more practical and integrational task of relating the significance of Jesus' life, death, and resurrection to everyday life.[25] One encounters in Paul's writings, perhaps better than anywhere else in the New Testament, someone who is consistently thinking through the practical implications of religious experience.

Engaging Scripture in an Academic Way

Claims to objectivity on the part of scholars concerning any academic subject are inevitably illusory in nature. All observers have biases that need to be acknowledged. In my own case, specific intellectual as well as religious sensibilities influence the kinds of questions I ask of the biblical text and likewise condition the answers I receive from them. Identifying as a scripture scholar, I employ the varied methods of modern critical scholarship in the attempt to honor the complexity inherent in the origin and function of the scriptural text. Partly this means that I take seriously what I regard as an evident fact: the writings of the New Testament are contingent texts. That is, they are the products of human beings who were shaped by the environment of the first-century Mediterranean world in which they lived. For this reason, I consider it necessary to interpret them in an academically responsible way. What is meant by "an academically responsible way" will be defined more clearly at the conclusion of this chapter. At this point, it is enough to note that this entails interpreting the writings of the New Testament against the background of their social, historical, and literary context.

At the same time, I consider that what these writings do best is to make religious claims about the person of Jesus and the shape of communal life that flows from these claims. I recognize that my own personality and education have influenced such a sensibility for focusing on the religious dimension of these texts. It is neither expected nor desired that readers share the viewpoint or conclusions advanced in this study. Working from the assumption that the New Testament is amenable to the application of a variety of academic

---

25. See Johnson, *The Real Jesus*, 119.

perspectives, this study articulates one voice in what ideally should be an ongoing conversation devoted to the task of the thoughtful interpretation of the texts of the New Testament. All manner of interpretation of the Bible, even academic interpretation, is inevitably shaped by one's own perspective; for that very reason it is both potentially insightful as well as potentially limited in terms of the conclusions it reaches. My modest hope is that in the pages to follow the balance will weigh more heavily toward the former than the latter.

The manner by which one goes about interpreting the writings of the New Testament cannot help but be influenced by the specific setting in which one encounters these texts. The experience of reading one of the New Testament Gospels, for example, will likely vary depending on whether one engages these writings in church, in an informal study group, or in the privacy of one's room. Each of these discrete settings also frequently elicits in distinctive ways the kinds of questions we raise in relation to the scriptural text. For example, an encounter with the text within the public setting of a church might entail simply listening to the passage recited as the prelude to a sermon. By contrast, informal study of the Bible with friends or even private reflection on a scriptural text might allow for a more personal meaning to be gained from the text.

Perhaps the most significant difference when it comes to interpreting biblical texts is between their study for personal, devotional purposes and the scholarly, disinterested approach of the academy. The latter approach is not in any way superior to the former; it is just different in terms of the kinds of questions it poses with respect to the text. When done well, a critical appraisal of the New Testament writings can allow for significant insight into the origin and purpose of these complex literary artifacts from a culture so different from our own.

The Academic Approach: Sensitivity to Historical, Cultural, and Literary Context

Foundational to the critical study of the New Testament is an appreciation for the historical, social, and cultural distance of these writings from the modern, post-industrial age. It is important to remember that the writings of the New Testament emerged within a context in which the ancient authors and their audiences shared similar cultural perspectives and expectations. That is, to borrow the terminology of Bruce Malina and Richard Rohrbaugh, the writings of the New Testament are the product of a "high context" society. Writings that come from high context societies, such as the world of Greco-Roman antiquity, take for granted that their audiences come to the text with a wealth of knowledge, values, and expectations already shared with the author.[26] For this reason ancient authors frequently introduced topics with little by way of explanation of details, details that modern readers often overlook.[27] As persons conditioned by present-day historical, cultural, and social norms, modern readers approaching these ancient texts do not recognize the unspoken assumptions, values, and experiences that ancient persons brought to their reading simply by virtue of their sharing the same cultural environment of ancient Mediterranean society. The result is often a misguided, if well-intentioned, interpretation.

An Example of the Academic Approach in Action: The Genre of the Gospels

In anticipation of the exploration of the New Testament Gospels beginning in the next chapter, the following observations pertaining to the genre of the Gospels might help to illustrate something of what is implied in an academic approach to the writings of the New Testament. Many scholars today contend that the Gospels most closely resemble a popular form of literature from the ancient world called a *bios* or, more simply, biography.[28] A *bios* was a narrative that focused on recounting in a chronological format the memorable words and deeds of significant persons such as famous philosophers, statesmen, or holy persons. A representative *bios* would be the *Life of Apollonius of Tyana* by Philostratus.[29] Most people probably

---

26. See Bruce J. Malina and Richard L. Rohrbaugh, *Social-Science Commentary on the Synoptic Gospels*, 2nd ed. (Minneapolis: Fortress, 2003), 11–12. See also, Leander E. Keck, *Taking the Bible Seriously*, 5th ed. (Nashville: Abingdon, 1981), 16–17.

27. Malina and Rohrbaugh, *Social-Science Commentary*, 11.

28. See Richard Burridge, *What Are the Gospels? A Comparison with Graeco-Roman Biography* (Grand Rapids: Eerdmans, 2004).

29. See Philostratus, *Life of Apollonius of Tyana*, ed. and trans. Christopher P. Jones, 4 vols., Loeb Classical Library (Cambridge, MA: Harvard University Press, 2005).

have definite ideas about what constitutes an effective biography of a notable person. For example, if one were to consider purchasing a biography of former President Barak Obama from a neighborhood Barnes and Noble, one would expect that the biographer had researched the topic thoroughly by consulting a variety of sources available for independent study by others. One would also expect the biography to be comprehensive in scope and to give ample attention to such details as the childhood of the future president, his personal triumphs and disappointments, and perhaps the ideals that shaped his philosophy of life and made him his own unique person. And while one would expect to encounter the author's own creative point of view, there would at the same time be every expectation that the biographer would strive to be as objective as possible in his or her assessment of the former president.

Ancient biographies diverged in important ways from the modern assumptions and expectations outlined above. First, such narratives were seldom comprehensive, preferring instead to showcase the general character of the notable person by focusing on the typical actions of that person. Second, although ancient authors frequently drew attention to the genealogical lineage of the biographical subject, extensive treatment of childhood events was rare.[30] Third, the primacy given in modern biographical narration to psychological development is almost completely absent in ancient biographical texts. Fourth, the principal concern of ancient biographers had less to do with realizing the goal of objectivity than with lavishing praise upon the biographical subject. Such praise had a very clear pedagogical purpose, which was to encourage ancient audiences to emulate the values and virtues of the biographical subject.

All these characteristics of ancient biography are also present in the Gospel portraits of the public ministry of Jesus. For example, the Gospels offer nothing like an exhaustive list of everything that Jesus did. Instead, the evangelists, reliant on their sources, edited those events that they considered most appropriate for their narrative aims. As already noted, the author of the Fourth Gospel is quite honest

---

30. John P. Meier observes that apart from truly significant historical figures little to nothing is known about the birth and childhood of most figures from the ancient world. See John P. Meier, *A Marginal Jew: Rethinking the Historical Jesus*, Anchor Bible Reference Library 1 (New York: Doubleday, 1991), 208.

with the reader about this: "Now Jesus did many other signs in the presence of his disciples, which are not written in this book" (John 20:30). Only two Gospels, Matthew and Luke, discuss anything about the origins of Jesus, and neither provides extensive details concerning Jesus' childhood. Did Jesus ever learn to read and write? What was his relationship with his family when he was growing up? Did Jesus grow in his awareness of his vocation? A tantalizing reference to the child Jesus growing in "wisdom" is found in the Gospel of Luke (Luke 2:52), yet the author reveals nothing of the content of this wisdom. These are all interesting questions, but unfortunately the Gospels do not supply any definite answers to them.

These observations are not raised with the intention of arguing that the Gospels do not preserve important memories of the kinds of things that Jesus said and did. At the same time, it is important to be mindful of the fact that the Gospels were not written with historical objectivity as their primary goal.[31] No literature coming down from the ancient world was written with such a goal in mind. The primary intention of each of the evangelists was to proclaim a message of salvation about a figure whom they saw as having ultimate or transcendent significance for their own lives as well as the lives of their audiences.

Summary

This chapter has offered the reader definitions of several important concepts that will inform this study. Key in this regard are the concepts of religious experience and common life as these concepts figure in the Gospels and the letters of Paul. Religious experience in this context has been described as the highly personal experience, given expression through religious proclamation, of the fundamental faith claim of the first Christians that Jesus was a living presence who embodied the ultimate purposes of God. In defining the concept of common life, it was emphasized that the writings of the New Testament tend to privilege the value of community as opposed to the value of individuality. Common life was defined as being

---

31. See Morna D. Hooker, *Beginnings: Keys That Open the Gospels* (Harrisburg, PA: Trinity, 1997), 2.

principally concerned with the living out in community of a highly personal faith commitment nurtured by religious experience. Lastly, the chapter supplied the reader with a broad sketch of the intellectual commitments that guide the approach taken in this book for the academic study of the New Testament.

Questions for Review

1. What is meant by the concept of religious experience?
2. What is meant by the concept of a common life?
3. Why are the terms *Christian* and *Christianity* problematic for describing the belief system and social makeup of the ancient audiences for the New Testament writings?
4. What do the designations "undisputed" and "disputed" mean in connection with the writings of the Apostle Paul?

Questions for Reflection

1. How does an academic approach help one to think about the nature of the differences between ancient and modern biographies?
2. Why is it important to consider the historical, sociological, and cultural distance of the writings of the New Testament from the modern, post-industrial setting?
3. Given that the Gospels do not attempt to offer objective history in the modern sense, do you think it is appropriate to draw upon them as historical sources, for example, for reconstructing a historical account of Jesus' life?

For Further Reading

Burridge, Richard. *What Are the Gospels? A Comparison with Graeco-Roman Biography*. Grand Rapids: Eerdmans, 2004.

Eliade, Mircea. *The Sacred and the Profane: The Nature of Religion*. Translated by Willard R. Trask. New York: Harcourt, 1959.

Gorman, Michael J. *Apostle of the Crucified Lord: A Theological Introduction to Paul and His Letters*. Grand Rapids: Eerdmans, 2002.

Hooker, M. D. *Beginnings: Keys That Open the Gospels*. Harrisburg, PA: Trinity, 1997.

Hugo, Victor. *Les Misérables*. Translated by Lee Fahnestock and Norman MacAfee. New York: Signet, 2013.

Johnson, Luke Timothy. *The Real Jesus: The Misguided Quest for the Historical Jesus and the Truth of the Traditional Gospels*. San Francisco: Harper One, 1996.

———. *Religious Experience in Earliest Christianity: A Missing Dimension in New Testament Studies*. Minneapolis: Fortress, 1998.

———. *The Writings of the New Testament: An Interpretation*. 3rd ed. Minneapolis: Fortress, 2010

Keck, Leander E. *Taking the Bible Seriously*. 5th ed. Nashville: Abingdon, 1981.

Koester, Craig R. *Symbolism in the Fourth Gospel: Meaning, Mystery, Community*. 2nd ed. Minneapolis: Fortress, 2003.

Malina, Bruce J., and Richard L. Rohrbaugh. *Social-Science Commentary on the Synoptic Gospels*. 2nd ed. Minneapolis: Fortress, 2003.

Meier, J. P. *A Marginal Jew: Rethinking the Historical Jesus*. Anchor Bible Reference Library 1. New York: Doubleday, 1991.

Moloney, Francis J. *The Gospel of John*. Edited by Daniel J. Harrington, SJ. Sacra Pagina 4. Collegeville, MN: Liturgical Press, 1998.

Orsi, Robert A. "Abundant History: Marian Apparitions as Alternative Modernity." In *Recent Themes in American Religious History: Historians in Conversation*, edited by Randall J. Stephens, 127–39. Columbia, SC: University of South Carolina Press, 2009.

Pascuzzi, Maria. *Paul: Windows on His Thought and His World*. Winona, MN: Anselm Academic, 2014.

Schneiders, Sandra. *The Revelatory Text: Interpreting the New Testament as Sacred Scripture*. San Francisco: Harper, 1991.

Smith, Jonathan Z. *Imagining Religion: From Babylon to Jonestown*. Chicago Studies in the History of Judaism. Chicago: University of Chicago Press, 1982.

Taves, Ann. *Revelatory Events: Three Case Studies of the Emergence of New Spiritual Paths*. Princeton: Princeton University Press, 2016.

Encountering Mark

The Way of Messiahship
and the Way of Discipleship

This investigation into the nature of religious experience and its relationship to the theme of common life begins with a consideration of the Gospel According to Mark.[1] The reader will recall the definition of religious experience established in the previous chapter. As is the case with the other Gospels, Mark's Gospel is written out of the religious experience that the Jesus who once lived, taught, suffered, and died is now alive in a new way and present to the audiences for whom the Gospels were first recorded. Mark's Gospel also witnesses to the creative interaction that invariably occurs in tandem with all human encounters with the transcendent. This creativity is illustrated both by Mark's presentation of Jesus as a suffering Messiah who serves others and in the implications that Mark draws from that depiction for a community attempting to define itself in a multicultural setting that was either indifferent or hostile to its religious commitments.

---

1. It is likely that all four canonical Gospels were originally anonymous texts that circulated without any names or titles attached to them. It was only later that the names Matthew, Mark, Luke, and John were added to these texts; exactly how much later is debated by scholars. The application of titles functioned at least in part as an attempt to distinguish these writings from other early gospels or gospel-like materials that were also in circulation. Scholars continue to use the names of those who were traditionally assumed to have been the authors of the four Gospels, not to assert the accuracy of the traditions but simply for convenience sake.

Placing Mark in Historical Context

While Mark is not the first Gospel one sees upon opening a modern English translation of the Bible, it was likely the first of the four Gospels to appear in writing, probably sometime around the year 70 CE. Little conclusive evidence exists for establishing either the date

The Metropolitan Museum of Art, Gift of J. Pierpont Morgan, 1917

Imagery from Ezekiel's vision of four "living creatures" before God's throne (Ezek. 1:5–11) was taken up in Christian iconography to represent the Four Gospels, as in this eleventh-century ivory plaque. The creature resembling a lion is associated with Mark's Gospel, and also represents Jesus' royal status.

or place of composition of Mark's Gospel. Scholars must look, therefore, for clues within the text that might reveal the author's knowledge of historical events known from other sources, such as the writings of the first-century CE Jewish historian Josephus. A traumatic experience for many first-century Jews was the fall of Jerusalem and destruction of the Temple in the year 70 CE, the decisive event of the Jewish War against Rome that began in 66 CE. Several passages in Mark's Gospel, notably 13:1–14, seem to exhibit an awareness of this event. Whether the Gospel was written sometime after the fall of the Temple or in anticipation of that event, however, cannot be established.[2]

Uncertainty also attends the question concerning the place of composition for Mark's Gospel. Wherever one locates Mark, however, it seems likely that the author was writing for a largely Gentile or non-Jewish audience. The author feels compelled, for example, to explain certain Jewish religious practices, which suggests that at least some segment of the audience was unfamiliar with them (see Mark 7:3–4; 14:2; 15:42). Moreover, Mark's frequent habit of translating Aramaic phrases (e.g., 3:17; 5:41; 7:11) suggests a Greek-speaking audience that was unfamiliar with that particular spoken dialect of Hebrew.[3] Mark's Gospel

---

2. See Jens Schröter, "The Gospel of Mark," in *The Blackwell Companion to the New Testament*, ed. David E. Aune (Chichester, UK; London; Malden, MA: Wiley Blackwell, 2010), 277–79.

3. Schröter, "The Gospel of Mark," 278.

also seems to envision a community that had either already experienced instances of suffering and persecution or anticipated such experiences in the future (see 13:9–13). Such exposure to persecution, perhaps in conjunction with anxiety prompted by the fall of the Temple, shapes the narrative of the public ministry of Jesus, the one whom Mark and his audience now view as the risen Lord. Literary evidence from outside the New Testament confirms that early Christian groups were persecuted in Rome during the time of the emperor Nero (68 CE)[4] and indeed church tradition dating back to at least the early third century CE associates Mark's Gospel with that capital city.[5] Other than Rome, there is little evidence for other sites of official persecution at this early stage in the church's history. That being said, Mark's Gospel really could have been written anywhere in the ancient Mediterranean world. Indeed, the author's evident concern for the effect of the fall of the Temple on his audience points just as strongly in favor of a location of composition in either Syria or Judea rather than Rome.[6]

© Joseph Calev / shutterstock.com

The Arch of Titus in Rome (81 CE) includes this panel portraying soldiers carrying the Temple's seven-branched menorah and other spoils from the fall of Jerusalem in 70 CE. The Jewish War was celebrated as a triumph in Rome; it was an unmitigated disaster for the people of Roman Palestine.

The Literary Achievement of Mark

When Mark's Gospel is read alongside the Gospels of Matthew and Luke it becomes evident that some kind of literary relationship exists

---

4. Tacitus, *Annals* 15:44.

5. Schröter, "The Gospel of Mark," 278.

6. Schröter, "The Gospel of Mark," 279.

among these three Gospels, which are known collectively as the Synoptic Gospels.[7] Most scholars today think that Mark's Gospel served as the primary template for the Gospels attributed to Matthew and Luke. These later evangelists copied much of the content of Mark, creatively adapting it in the process, while at the same time supplementing Mark with materials such as birth accounts, resurrection appearance stories, and traditions that focused on Jesus' role as a teacher.[8] Upon first reading Mark, students sometimes express misgivings over what might be called the literary achievement of the author. Mark's writing style appears simplistic and repetitive, and his transitions between episodes appear abrupt, even clumsy. A bit like a toddler on a playground, Mark seems to jump from one story to the next, leaving the reader with the uncomfortable feeling of wishing the author had lingered just a bit longer on any one given story. Such impressions are only strengthened when Mark is read alongside the comparatively polished Gospels of Matthew and Luke.

Reactions such as these to a perceived roughness in Mark reveal potential clues regarding the process by which this Gospel may have come into being. Although the four Gospels read as if they are complete and finished narratives, the precise process by which the traditions contained in them emerged and took final form is not entirely clear. Given the high rate of illiteracy that existed in the ancient world, it is probable that the majority—though certainly not all—of the memories of the events of Jesus' life and death circulated orally for decades prior to being included in the written Gospels, beginning with the Gospel of Mark. Mark's Gospel certainly reads like a coherent narrative with consistent thematic elements and literary devices lending a holistic tenor to the story. It is quite probable that the memories of the words and deeds of Jesus circulated in both written and oral formats from the very beginning. Over time brief collections of stories coalesced into separate written compilations, with the process finally

---

7. Derived from the combination of a Greek proposition and Greek verb, the term *synoptic* translates as "to see alongside of."

8. The modern Two-Source Hypothesis posits that the authors of Matthew and Luke independently copied Mark while at the same time making use of a now lost source that contained mostly sayings of Jesus. This hypothetical source is designated Q, from the German word *Quelle* ("source"). See John R. Donahue, SJ, and Daniel J. Harrington, SJ, *The Gospel of Mark*, ed. Daniel J. Harrington, SJ, Sacra Pagina 2 (Collegeville, MN: Liturgical Press, 2002), 4.

leading to Mark who, as far as we know, crafted the first extended written narrative of the life, death, and resurrection of Jesus.[9]

While traces of the elusive backstory of the Jesus traditions are difficult to discern in Mark's Gospel, it is clear that Mark is a highly intentional author, who exercises substantial creative control over the traditions he has inherited.[10] Mark is especially adept at arranging inherited materials in thematically creative ways. For example, Mark highlights the activity of Jesus as a miracle-worker in the first four chapters of his narrative, beginning with an account of a dramatic exorcism (Mark 1:23–28) and ending with an equally dramatic account of Jesus calming a storm at sea (4:35–41). Students are sometimes surprised to learn that the kind of miracle-working activity Mark ascribes to Jesus would not necessarily have made Jesus appear unique to his contemporaries. Ancient sources from both the Jewish as well as the Greco-Roman world provide numerous parallels to many of Jesus' recorded miracles.[11] Perhaps realizing this, Mark prefaces his account of the extraordinary abilities of Jesus with an episode that supplies an interpretive lens for glimpsing what Mark sees as the deeper import of the miracles performed by Jesus: "Now after John was arrested, Jesus came to Galilee, proclaiming the good news of God, and saying, 'The time is fulfilled, and the kingdom of God has come near; repent, and believe in the good news'" (1:14–15). As teachers point out in literature classes, it can prove useful when examining texts to attend to the beginnings of stories, since it is frequently at the commencement of a narrative where elements crucial to effective storytelling appear, elements such as plot, characterization, and setting.[12] The New

---

9. See E. P. Sanders, *The Historical Figure of Jesus* (London: Penguin, 1993), 58–60.

10. Since female authors were extremely rare in the ancient world, it is likely that this Gospel's author was a man. But this should not be taken as established fact. As already noted, Mark's Gospel is anonymous. It is therefore impossible to know the gender of the real author.

11. Important examples from the Jewish Scriptures would include the narratives associated with the Jewish prophets Elijah and Elisha. Closer to the time of Jesus are the Jewish charismatic holy men Honi the Circle Drawer and Hanina ben Dosa. A particularly notable example of a first-century CE wonder-worker from the Greco-Roman world would be the philosopher and holy man Apollonius of Tyana.

12. See Francis J. Moloney, *The Gospel of Mark: A Commentary* (Peabody, MA: Hendrickson, 2002), 27. A particularly good introduction for the appreciation of the Gospel of Mark as a creative story can be found in Elizabeth Struthers Malbon, *Hearing Mark: A Listener's Guide* (Harrisburg, PA: Trinity, 2002).

Testament Gospels are no exception in this regard. The passage from Mark's Gospel quoted above serves both to conclude the introduction or prologue to Mark's Gospel (Mark 1:1–13) and to introduce the reader to the first words of the story's principal character: Jesus. Jesus announces that the beginning of his public ministry coincides with a special moment in time in which the power of God's rule is becoming manifest in the world.

The precise wording of Jesus' announcement concerning the kingdom is, however, ambiguous. On the one hand, Jesus declares

The Narrative Flow of Mark

Prologue (1:1-13)
Jesus the Beloved Son
Appearance of John the Baptist; baptism and testing of Jesus.

First Division (1:14–8:21)
The In-Breaking of the Kingdom
Proclamation concerning the coming kingdom and call of first disciples; initial healings; series of five conflict stories with religious leaders; mysterious teaching in parables; miracle at sea; more healings, feedings, a second sea miracle; conflicts with enemies and his own disciples.

Second Division (8:22-10:52)
Lessons on Discipleship
First story of the healing of a blind person; Peter's confession; teaching an alternative model of power; second and final story of a healing of a blind person.

Third Division (11:1-16:8)
God's Son Revealed in Suffering, Death, and Vindication
Arrival in Jerusalem; disturbance at the Temple flanked by cursing and withering of a fig tree; controversies in the Temple; the widow's offering; predictions about the end; anointing at Bethany and Judas's decision for betrayal; final tragic scenes with disciples and accounts of betrayal; arrest, interrogation, Peter's denial, execution, and burial; account of empty tomb.

that the "time is fulfilled," seemingly implying that the kingdom is a present reality. On the other hand, the language about the kingdom drawing "near" highlights the futurity of the kingdom. Adding to the complexity is the fact that the Gospels frequently portray Jesus as holding both these emphases in tension. As Mark describes it, God's kingdom is both a transcendent reality that will transform the world in the age to come and at the same time the power of God's rule that is already mysteriously present in the public ministry of Jesus.

Mark's Good News: Glimpses of the Theme of Common Life and Initial Reflections on the Identity of Jesus

When placed alongside the other Gospels in the New Testament, Mark's Gospel presents a distinctive, even disorienting reading experience. In contrast to Matthew and Luke, Mark gives no information at all regarding the birth and childhood of Jesus, preferring instead to begin the narrative with Jesus already as a grown man (Mark 1:9). Missing also from Mark are any episodes where the risen Jesus appears to his followers after being raised from the dead.[13] The omission of such narrative bookends serves the purpose of drawing the attention of the reader to the account of the public ministry of Jesus and especially to the conflictual relationship that exists between Jesus and his disciples.

In some ways, the disciples in Mark appear as ideal adherents; this is seen initially in their eagerness to abandon everything in response to the summons of Jesus to follow him (Mark 1:16–20; 10:28). But at the same time, the Gospel shows that the disciples embody many of the unvarnished traits that characterize all human beings, at least to varying degrees. Thus the disciples show themselves to be envious (10:41), power hungry (9:33–34), fearful (4:40), even vindictive (9:38; 10:13). They are obstinately obtuse, on several occasions almost intentionally so (4:13; 8:4, 16–21). While it is possible that this depiction is historically accurate, the depths to which

---

13. Mark does, however, have an account of an empty tomb, a detail found in all four Gospels. There is wide scholarly consensus that Mark's Gospel originally ended at 16:8 with the story of the discovery of an empty tomb. Verses 9–20, where resurrection appearances are found, were added to Mark's Gospel by later copyists.

the disciples' failures descend make it somewhat more likely that on display here is the artistry of Mark as a storyteller.[14] But if this is the case, what might have motivated Mark to cast the disciples in such a poor light? Although a definitive explanation remains elusive, a partial answer emerges if we think of Mark less as an impartial historian and more as a creative narrator; a narrator who sees his role, moreover, as not simply that of a storyteller, but as a shaper of communal identity. By depicting the disciples in such an unflattering way, Mark invites readers to imagine a different model of common life, one that is exemplified not by patterns of human dysfunctionality but by the values of the kingdom of God that are embodied and exemplified by Jesus throughout the events of his historical ministry.

Mark introduces the theme of common life in the context of his account of the call of the first disciples: Simon, Andrew, James, and John:

> As Jesus passed along the Sea of Galilee, he saw Simon and his brother Andrew casting a net into the sea—for they were fishermen. And Jesus said to them, "Follow me and I will make you fish for people." And immediately they left their nets and followed him. As he went a little farther, he saw James son of Zebedee and his brother John, who were in their boat mending the nets. Immediately he called them; and they left their father Zebedee in the boat with the hired men, and followed him. (Mark 1:16–20)

Many students, when invited to share their reactions to this passage, respond that the scene strikes them as completely unrealistic. Why would these men leave behind their livelihood and family as a result of a single phrase uttered by someone whom they have never met before? What makes the episode even stranger, even a bit unsettling to some, is the puzzling nature of the summons. Fishing for people? What kind of incentive is that? Its meaning certainly does not seem clear enough to warrant leaving everything behind to follow someone who at this point in the story offers only a challenging metaphor!

---

14. The disciples give a particularly poor showing when it comes to their perceiving the significance of the two feeding stories (see Mark 8:11–21).

The episode of the call of the first disciples might well preserve an important historical memory about Jesus: he appears to have held an unusually high estimation of the personal role he was to play in what he perceived as God's unfolding intentions for history. He even cautions his disciples that on the day of judgment a person's fate will be determined solely on the measure of how that person responded to him and his teachings (Mark 8:38). In several of the stories that comprise the opening chapters of the Gospel, Mark repeatedly emphasizes the immense authority of Jesus. For example, in his capacity as the "the Holy One of God" (1:24) Jesus expels demons; he reveals intimate knowledge of the willingness of God to forgive sin, an admission that strikes his opponents as a supreme example of overreach (2:5–7); he defends an apparent Sabbath infraction by placing himself on a higher status than King David (2:25–26); and most provocatively of all, Jesus applies to himself the title of "Son of Man" (2:10, 28; 14:62). This mysterious title, which appears to have been Jesus' preferred self-designation, is open to various translations, and for that reason it remains ambiguous as to its precise meaning. While Jesus may have used the title to refer to his status as a human being, the title may also have reminded some of his contemporaries of that mysterious figure from the book of Daniel called the Son of Man.[15] If, as Morna Hooker suggests, the Son of Man figure in Daniel functions as a corporate image representative of the Jewish people, Jesus may have viewed himself as fulfilling that role through his public ministry.[16] Whatever may have been Jesus' intention in using this title, he seldom appears in Mark's Gospel as someone who had confidence issues! That is not to assume that every detail found in the examples noted above is historical. The point made here is simply that, as Mark portrays him, Jesus seems to have been quite self-assured about the importance of his vocation. He clearly saw himself as a spokesperson for, as well as an agent of, God.

As so often happens in the Gospels, Mark's account of the call of the first disciples challenges the reader to find meaning in a story that is fundamentally disorienting. As already noted, Mark's Gospel

---

15. See Morna Hooker, *The Gospel According to Saint Mark*, Black's New Testament Commentary (Peabody, MA: Hendrickson, 1997), 89–90.

16. Hooker, *The Gospel According to Saint Mark*, 90–91.

is a creative and engaging story. And like all good stories the Gospel invites the reader to enter its world and emerge transformed in some way.[17] The call episode is highly self-contained and in principle could have been placed someplace else in the narrative.[18] Mark, however, intentionally positions the scene after Jesus' dramatic notice concerning the dawning kingdom of God (Mark 1:15). In this way, Mark crafts a powerful statement regarding the communal significance of God's rule: the dawning kingdom of God is not a private phenomenon; instead it is the kind of reign that requires a community of a particular sort if the kingdom is to become embodied in the world.[19]

The call narrative demonstrates that the common life summoned into existence by Jesus upsets traditional social commitments. Simon and Andrew abandon their inherited vocations as fishermen to forge new relationships with persons with whom they have no biological ties. More dramatic still, the theme of the severing of the bond with family, merely hinted at in the actions of Simon and Andrew, becomes flagrant when James and John abandon their father in the boat. Ironically the only persons who remain committed to the elder Zebedee are the hired laborers, the very ones without any biological tie to him whatsoever.

Subsequent episodes in Mark's narrative flesh out more details of this common life. Gender inclusiveness, for example, is a hallmark of this community. Given the patriarchal structure of ancient Mediterranean society, it is noteworthy that women play a significant role in Mark's Gospel as devoted followers of Jesus,[20] even to the point of modeling how an authentic disciple should act. For example, women followers, not male followers, accompany Jesus to the place of his

---

17. Elizabeth Struthers Malbon summarizes this point well: "The Gospel is not a simple history book. And it's not neutral. It's written from the persuaded to be persuasive." *Hearing Mark*, 4.

18. In contrast to Mark, Luke places the call story not after the baptism but after Jesus' return to his hometown of Nazareth (see Luke 5:1–11).

19. Malbon, *Hearing Mark*, 17.

20. Many scholars consider that the term *disciple* is an appropriate title for Jesus' female followers despite the fact that Mark never explicitly identifies any woman as a disciple. While Jesus' inner circle of "the Twelve" consists of only male disciples, it is the female followers of Jesus who generally do a better job of modelling behavior that characterizes authentic discipleship.

execution, witness his burial, and visit his tomb (Mark 15:40–16:3). Mark describes these women—several of whom are named—who witness the death of Jesus as "follow[ing]" him (15:41), employing the identical Greek verb he used to describe how Andrew and Simon "followed" Jesus (1:18). Similarly, Mark associates women disciples with the act of serving (1:31; 15:41); although the term never appears in connection with the male disciples, Jesus describes the act of serving as the principal vocation of his life: "The Son of Man came not to be served but to serve, and to give his life a ransom for many" (10:45). The only character in Mark's narrative who ever teaches Jesus anything is a woman, identified by Mark as a Gentile; Jesus, in turn rewards her for her insight by healing her daughter (7:24–30). This is not to say that every mention of women in Mark's Gospel is favorable. Women are implicated in the execution of John the Baptist (6:17–29), and the Gospel famously concludes with women fleeing the tomb just as the male disciples fled when Jesus was arrested in the garden (16:8; cf. 14:50). Women are not included among the Twelve (3:13–19), nor do they appear in the scene of Jesus' final meal (14:22–31). Moreover, Jesus is not exactly egalitarian, as much as we, as modern readers, might want him to be; he is very clearly the recognized leader of the community, and feels free to give orders to his followers (6:8). All this is simply to say that Mark's Gospel reflects the complexity of women's roles and status in ancient society.

Returning to the call narrative, it is reasonable to suppose that the actual details of the historical encounter that Jesus had with his first followers were more complex than is implied by this tightly compressed story. It is, however, precisely the artificial features of the incident that provokes the reader to search for an interpretation that transcends the merely historical.[21] Prompted by Mark's literary creativity, readers are left with the impression that a kingdom without

---

21. For those who are new to the academic study of the New Testament, one of the more difficult concepts to grasp is the distinction that scholars make between historical analysis of the New Testament and New Testament Studies. With regard to the Gospels, the former is concerned with the attempt to reconstruct historically Jesus' self-understanding and what he actually said and did while the latter focuses on interpreting the unique theological interpretation of Jesus found in each of the Gospels. While the two approaches can inform one another, it is important to notice their distinctive aims. See Mark Alan Powell, *Introducing the New Testament: A Historical, Literary, and Theological Survey* (Grand Rapids: Eerdmans, 2009), 70–72.

a community is no kingdom at all and that the models of community that are familiar today may not, in fact, fit the kind of common life envisioned by God. This is less a historical observation about the past than it is an invitation by Mark to the reader to reimagine the present, and the shape of common life within it, in another way.

The Identity of Jesus in Mark

Mark develops further the theme of common life by linking it to reflections concerning the deeper identity of Jesus. Mark has already identified Jesus in the opening line of the Gospel as the "Christ" and "Son of God" (Mark 1:1). Both titles should be understood against the background of the Jewish Scriptures, what contemporary Christians call the Old Testament. "Christ" comes from the Greek term *Christos*, meaning "anointed one." As such, it corresponds to the Hebrew term *Mashiach*, from which the term "Messiah" comes. Various types of persons were anointed in the Jewish Scriptures, most notably kings, prophets, and priests. To be anointed was to be set apart—typically in a ceremonial setting—for a special task or service before the God of Israel. As such, the term originally bore a functional as opposed to a personal meaning.[22] In calling Jesus the "Christ," Mark confers upon Jesus an especially honorable vocation: Jesus is the agent of God, authorized by God to work on God's behalf.

Jesus as Son of God

The title "Son of God" is somewhat more problematic. Does Mark attempt to identify Jesus as a divine being? Answering this question in the affirmative might seem natural given what many Christians today believe about Jesus. But approaching this question from an academic perspective, it must be remembered that Mark is not a contemporary Christian looking back over thousands of years of Christian theological reflection. Surprisingly few texts in the New Testament explicitly identify Jesus as divine. What significance, then, might this title have had for Mark? The Jewish background to the title might provide a clue. In the Jewish Scriptures the Jewish king

---

22. See Alan F. Segal, *Rebecca's Children: Judaism and Christianity in the Roman World* (Cambridge, MA: Harvard University Press, 1986), 64–65.

was sometimes identified as God's son (e.g., Ps. 2:7). This usage, like "anointed," again highlights the idea of agency. "Son" of God also appears in the Jewish Scriptures with an important communal significance, as when the Jewish people are designated as God's Son in a collective sense (see Hos. 11:1).

In light of this scriptural background, it seems reasonable to say that Mark applies the title of Son to Jesus primarily in a relational sense. That is, by calling Jesus Son of God, Mark highlights Jesus' fundamental stance of obedience before God. For Mark, Jesus is that unique human being who is perfectly committed to God's cause and completely transparent to God's will. One of the best places to see this relational understanding of sonship is in the passage where Jesus prays to God on the night of his arrest: "And going a little farther, he threw himself on the ground and prayed that, if it were possible, the hour might pass from him. He said 'Abba, Father, for you all things are possible; remove this cup from me; yet, not what I want, but what you want'" (Mark 14:35–36). Contemplating the likelihood of his suffering and death, Jesus struggles to align his will to the will of the one whom he identifies as his Father.[23] Paul says much the same about Jesus in his Letter to the Philippians, where he notes that Jesus was "obedient to the point of death" (Phil. 2:8). On this same point, we might also refer to the Letter to the Hebrews, where the anonymous author says of Jesus, "Although he was a Son, he learned obedience through what he suffered" (Heb. 5:8). It should be noted that in this particular passage the author of Hebrews explicitly links the title of Son to the concept of obedience. As applied to Jesus, then, the terminology of sonship gives expression to the early Christian faith affirmation that Jesus fully aligned his will to the will of God. Likely lurking in the background of this faith affirmation is another facet of Jesus' Jewish background: the concept of covenant righteousness, which has everything to do with living one's life in accordance with the will of God as revealed in Torah.[24] The topic of righteousness

---

23. A particularly powerful contemporary illustration of this relational meaning of sonship can be found in Nikos Kazantzakis's novel, *The Last Temptation of Christ*, trans. P. A. Bien (New York: Simon and Schuster, 1998).

24. The Hebrew word *Torah*, while often translated as "law," is actually best translated as "guidance" or "instruction."

and its connection to the idea of covenant will be explored in more depth in the next chapter dealing with the Gospel of Matthew.

The Role of Suffering in the Identity of Jesus

Of all the Gospels, Mark is the one that most accentuates the importance of the events of the suffering and death of Jesus for understanding the deeper meaning of Jesus' identity. Although the explicit narration of Jesus' final days does not appear until chapter fourteen of the Gospel, signs of the impending arrest and execution of Jesus appear early in the narrative and lend a tragic texture to the activities of Jesus as a miracle-worker and teacher. Overall, the opening chapters of Mark convey to the reader an auspicious tone to the beginning of Jesus' public ministry; through his many acts of healing, Jesus powerfully embodies the liberating power of the kingdom of God and receives popular acclaim. Complementing the many accounts of physical healings, Mark also presents Jesus engaging in activities that make space for what we might call acts of social healing:

> And as he sat at dinner in Levi's house, many tax collectors and sinners were also sitting with Jesus and his disciples— for there were many who followed him. When the scribes of the Pharisees saw that he was eating with sinners and tax collectors, they said to his disciples, "Why does he eat with tax collectors and sinners?" When Jesus heard this, he said to them, "Those who are well have no need of a physician, but those who are sick; I have come to call not the righteous but sinners." (Mark 2:15–17)

In this scene Mark shows that communal reconciliation is part of what it means for Jesus to embody God's kingdom in the world. Within the narrative world of the Gospel the labels "sinner" and "tax collector" function essentially as social deviancy labels. That is, they identify persons who act in self-serving ways that expose a lack of concern for, or love of, one's neighbor.[25] Aware that the customary

---

25. See Amy Jill Levine, *Short Stories by Jesus: The Enigmatic Parables of a Controversial Rabbi* (New York: Harper One, 2014), 33–34.

communal response to such persons would be to disassociate from them, Jesus takes a more complicated but potentially more creative stance. He chooses to share table fellowship with such persons and, in this way, enacts in concrete ways the priority he places on communal and individual reconciliation. Jesus' assumption, apparently, is that it is only by drawing near to such persons that reconciliation between all members of society can become possible.

Jesus' actions provoke significant discomfort, however, among the scribes of the Pharisees, since his behavior challenges assumptions regarding the appropriate limits or boundaries of legitimate community. Mark wants his readers to feel uncomfortable as well. The "sinners" of this story need only to be updated for the episode to pose a challenge to contemporary readers. Would we celebrate or instead feel resentment about a paroled convict participating in the communal civic right of voting in a political primary or general election? Or on an even more personal level, would we want to work alongside such a person or even carpool with him or her on the way to work? We begin to notice that woven throughout the various acts of physical and social healing that characterize the first days of Jesus' public ministry are narrative hints pointing to the inevitable suffering and death of Jesus. The most obvious use of foreshadowing in this regard appears in a series of stories found in Mark 2:1–3:6. Centering on the escalating antagonism between Jesus and the scribes and Pharisees, this collection of five conflict stories culminates with the decision of the scribes, Pharisees, and the officials of Herod to annihilate Jesus in response to his having healed a man with a paralyzed hand on the Sabbath (3:6).

The conflict stories raise some important considerations concerning the relationship of Jesus to his native Judaism. Far from encountering a figure who repudiates his Jewish heritage, Jesus, according to Mark, fully embraces that heritage. For example, Jesus once again makes an appearance in the synagogue (Mark 3:1), the ancient Jewish version of a modern day community center, where prayer and study of the Jewish Law also took place. Like other Jews of his day, Jesus takes seriously the observance of the Sabbath in a way that honors the mandated day of rest (2:23–28; 3:1–4). Jesus points not to himself, but to the God of Israel as the source of the forgiveness of sins granted to the crippled man (2:5).[26] Even the customary table fellowship of Jesus points to an important aspect of the symbolic world of Judaism, namely, the conviction that the age to come will be like a savory banquet where everyone is invited to the celebration.[27] These passages complement many others in Mark where Jesus demonstrates deep investment in Jewish religious traditions. For example, in the story of the healing of the leper (1:40–45) Jesus upholds Jewish purity legislation by directing the now-healed leper to show himself to the priest (1:44). Jesus similarly regards the Jewish Law or Torah as the divinely mandated guide for living a life of righteousness before God (10:19; 12:28–31).

In recounting these stories, however, historical reminiscence is not the primary concern of Mark. Tellingly, the episodes appear arranged in a somewhat artificial manner that serves to dramatize escalating tension between Jesus and the learned figures of the Jewish community. The resulting decision to kill Jesus is dramatic and unrealistic at the same time. As E. P. Sanders persuasively argues, the kinds of debates presented in these stories were not in fact matters of life and death for most Jews.[28] There was room for debate about how to observe the Sabbath and Jews presumably did not contemplate murder over someone's choice of dinner guests. Although the culmination of the conflict stories is historically unrealistic, the stories do serve Mark's larger narrative purposes by anticipating the climax of the narrative: the suffering and death of Jesus. Moreover, the conflict

---

26. The voice of the Greek verb for forgiveness employed by Mark is passive: "your sins are forgiven," implying that God is the direct agent of the forgiveness.

27. Levine, *Short Stories*, 13. I am using the term "symbolic world" in the sense employed by Luke Timothy Johnson. A symbolic world refers to the shared concepts and meanings that define the way a community conceptualizes and gives meaning to its existence primarily within the context of narratives. See Luke Timothy Johnson, *The Writings of the New Testament: An Interpretation*, 3rd ed. (Minneapolis: Fortress, 2010), 10–11.

28. Sanders, *The Historical Figure of Jesus*, 130. One might legitimately ask: What accounts for the fact that Jesus was eventually killed? As one might expect, this is an enormously complex question to answer. I share the view that Jesus' actions with respect to the Temple in Jerusalem likely played the most important role in the events leading to his eventual arrest and execution. Indeed, there are passages in the Gospels that imply that some saw Jesus as making some kind of threat against the Temple (Matt. 26:60–61; Mark 14:58; John 2:19). Interestingly, all of these passages suggest that Jesus looked forward to a time when a new temple would replace the former one.

stories introduce a theme to be developed later in the narrative relating to Jesus' status as Son of God and Messiah. As readers arrive at Mark 3:6, they become aware for the first time that the one who is committed to embodying God's kingdom will innocently suffer for that commitment. Up to this point in the Gospel, all the signs of the kingdom have been signs of power and the promise of renewed life. Mark's Gospel is becoming darker and will become darker still.

Mark's Jesus Redefines Family

Following the account of the healing of the man with the paralyzed hand (Mark 3:1–6) are a series of stories in which the theme of common life receives further thematic refinement. Once more the disciples figure prominently, as Jesus appoints twelve followers to serve as a special inner group. By positioning the appointment of the Twelve beside two seemingly unrelated stories, Mark crafts a particularly challenging statement about the nature of common life. The action opens with a note that Jesus "went home" (3:19), which is likely meant to remind the reader of the home of Simon and Andrew in Capernaum.[29] In quick succession we meet Jesus' mother, his siblings, and a group of scribes from Jerusalem. It is a tense scene. Mark informs the reader that Jesus' family considered him to be mentally

Significance of the Twelve

The appointment of the Twelve likely held symbolic significance for the historical Jesus. Only two of the original twelve tribes of Israel (Judah and Benjamin) remained in existence during the period of Jesus' public ministry. Some Jews of this period hoped that God would reassemble the lost tribes in some miraculous manner at the close of the age (see Jer. 3:6-12; 30:3). If Jesus also embraced this hope, he may have appointed the Twelve with the intention of associating his ministry with what he believed to be the dawning of that longed-for miracle.

---

29. John R. Donahue, SJ, and Daniel J. Harrington, SJ, *The Gospel of Mark*, ed. Daniel J. Harrington, SJ, Sacra Pagina 2 (Collegeville, MN: Liturgical Press, 2002), 93.

unbalanced (3:21). The scribal leaders from Jerusalem express a far less sympathetic estimation: they classify Jesus as a religious deviant who conducts exorcisms under the influence of demonic authority (3:22). It is a clever accusation. Unable to deny that Jesus can expel demons, the religious authorities instead try to undermine Jesus' authority by calling into question the source of his power. Apparently stung by the charge, Jesus forcibly responds,

> How can Satan cast out Satan? If a kingdom is divided against itself, that kingdom cannot stand. And if a house is divided against itself, that house will not be able to stand. And if Satan has risen up against himself and is divided, he cannot stand, but his end has come. But no one can enter a strong man's house and plunder his property without first tying up the strong man; then indeed the house can be plundered. (Mark 3:23–27)

Jesus' point is that he cannot be an exorcist who curtails Satan's power by liberating demon-possessed people and simultaneously a servant of demonic power. For those with the eyes to see, it is the power of the God of Israel that Jesus channels. Jesus then proceeds to accuse the scribes of offending God's honor as a result of their accusation (Mark 3:28–30). If chapter 3 had concluded with this episode, the scene would have effectively complemented the intense hostility between Jesus and the religious authorities already on display in the conflict stories (2:1–3:6). Instead, Mark proceeds to this final interaction between Jesus and his family:

> Then his mother and his brothers came; and standing outside, they sent to him and called him. A crowd was sitting around him; and they said to him, "Your mother and your brothers and sisters are outside, asking for you." And he replied, "Who are my mother and my brothers?" And looking at those who sat around him, he said, "Here are my mother and my brothers! Whoever does the will of God is my brother and sister and mother." (Mark 3:31–35)

The careful reader will notice that Mark has taken two originally separate stories and merged them. Such blending of stories constitutes one of Mark's favorite narrative tools for engaging in theological reflection: the intercalation technique. In this example, the technique, which constitutes a kind of literary sandwich, begins with the appearance of the family of Jesus who accuse him of mental instability (Mark 3:20–21). Mark then transitions to a separate incident where, in response to the accusation that he works under demonic influence, Jesus accuses the scribes of dishonoring God (3:22–30). Finally, Mark returns to the first scene by revisiting Jesus' mother and siblings (3:31–35). Mark obviously wants the reader to make a connection between the two stories. The problem is that it is not immediately apparent what that connection might be. In fact, it appears as if Mark wants to challenge the reader to puzzle over a variety of possible interpretations.

It seems clear enough that both stories illustrate the theme of opposition to Jesus. What is surprising, however, is that in one the stories the opposition comes not from outsiders, but from insiders: Jesus' family. One could perhaps make a persuasive argument that the charges levelled against Jesus in the two stories are different. While his family merely imputes madness to Jesus, the religious authorities pronounce a more hostile accusation: Jesus is in league with demons. The religious authorities, therefore, seem to be more culpable. But does Mark see it this way? Might the intercalation be functioning to suggest that any form of opposition to Jesus is opposition to the kingdom, even opposition to God? Alternatively, in view of the proximity of the intercalation to the account of the appointing of the Twelve, perhaps Mark subtly foreshadows even more failures to come on the part of the Twelve? From one perspective, the disciples constitute members of the new family of Jesus; but if it is possible for the biological family of Jesus to find themselves suddenly on the outside, is it possible for the disciples to become outsiders too?

These reflections are merely possible interpretations. Mark appears perfectly comfortable with letting the reader wrestle with the meaning of this particular instance of intercalation without providing any sort of definitive closure. That said, since the intercalation concludes with Jesus redefining a true family member as someone who does the will of God, it would seem that Mark is making some kind of application to the theme of common life. What might this application have been? It is quite possible that at least some among the original audience for Mark's Gospel may have lost a great deal as a consequence of their conversion to the Gospel message. Such persons might potentially see their own experience with familial alienation mirrored in Jesus' words.[30] But something more seems to be at stake. The early chapters of Mark portray Jesus as the agent of God who embodies the will of God. These chapters also describe significant resistance to the will of God as illustrated in the conflict stories and in the example of the intercalation just analyzed. As a creative storyteller, Mark employs the themes of resistance and opposition to Jesus in an effort to link the identity of Jesus to his eventual fate of suffering and death. It would seem that Mark is doing something similar with the concept of common life in the sense that he wants the reader to see that the identity of Jesus has implications for the character of the community that gathers around him. But what would a community look like that took Jesus as its model? What behaviors would inform its common life?

Common Life in Response to the Way of Messiahship

Arguably the most dramatic episode in the Gospel of Mark occurs just as Jesus and his disciples prepare to make their way to Jerusalem, the city where Jesus will be handed over to his enemies:

> Jesus went on with his disciples to the villages of Caesarea Philippi; and on the way he asked his disciples, "Who do people say that I am?" And they answered him, "John the Baptist; and others, Elijah; and still others, one of the prophets." He asked them, "But who do you say that I am?" Peter answered him, "You are the Messiah." And he sternly ordered them not to tell anyone about him." (Mark 8:27–30)

After questioning his disciples concerning his status among the general populace, Jesus challenges the disciples to articulate for themselves what they personally think of him. Taking the initiative,

---

30. Malbon, *Hearing Mark*, 28.

Peter declares Jesus to be the Messiah. This is a decisive moment in the story, since up until this point in the narrative the only characters who have recognized Jesus' identity as Messiah and Son of God have been the demons that Jesus vanquishes (Mark 3:11). As already noted, the concept of Messiah is closely associated with the idea of agency. A Messiah or "anointed one" designates someone who is set apart to work on God's behalf. But as the narrative proceeds it appears that Peter has either someone or something more specific in mind when he identifies Jesus with this title:

> Then he began to teach them that the Son of Man must undergo great suffering, and be rejected by the elders, the chief priests, and the scribes, and be killed, and after three days rise again. He said all this quite openly. And Peter took him aside and began to rebuke him. But turning and looking at his disciples, he rebuked Peter and said, "Get behind me, Satan! For you are setting your mind not on divine things but on human things." (Mark 8:31–33)

Given its dramatic tension, this interaction between Jesus and Peter is evidently meant to be taken as a key moment in the narrative. Curiously, Jesus deflects the Messiah title given him by Peter in favor of another title, the Son of Man. Jesus remarks that a glorious destiny awaits this figure, since he will be vindicated by God. Prior to this experience of vindication, however, will be the far darker experience of profound rejection and suffering for the Son of Man. With his response, Jesus seems to be trying to clarify in what sense he is the Messiah. But since Mark does not clarify what Peter explicitly has in mind when he calls Jesus the Messiah, readers are left wondering about the precise significance that the title has for Peter.

One popular interpretation is that Peter thinks of the Messiah as a military figure, someone who will fight on behalf of the Jewish people as a sort of warrior king. This was certainly one concept of the Messiah that would have been available in the period. But it was not the only one. Indeed, the diversity of messianic models current in the period makes it difficult to know for certain just how widespread or normative was a militaristic understanding of the Messiah. As E. P. Sanders notes, in the relatively few Jewish sources that are relevant for this period where a Messiah figure does appear that figure notably does not personally engage in warfare.[31] One might reasonably wonder, however, whether either Peter or Mark may still have viewed Jesus as a royal figure. Already the observation has been made that Jewish kings constituted one of the classes of persons who were traditionally anointed. Moreover, the Gospel narratives preserve suggestive passages where the issue of the possible royal status of Jesus is considered. Thus in all four Gospels the Roman governor Pontius Pilate pointedly asks Jesus if he is a king (Matt. 27:11; Mark 15:2; Luke 23:3; John 18:33). Jesus gives an evasive response to Pilate according to each of the four accounts.[32] These passages become even more suggestive when they are considered in light of the fact that in all four Gospels Jesus was crucified precisely as "King of the Jews" (Matt. 27:37; Mark 15:26; Luke 23:38; John 19:19).[33]

Did the disciples and the crowds see Jesus as quite possibly a royal figure? Did Pilate think of Jesus in this way or was he merely concerned with what he saw as a dangerous popular perception—that Jesus was a king in the eyes of the Jerusalem populace? Does Mark think of Jesus as a king? If so, what kind of a king is he? And perhaps the most provocative question of all: Did Jesus think of himself as a king? The prevalence of royal language in Mark is certainly extensive enough to pose all these questions even if conclusive answers to them remain elusive.

Although one could certainly argue that Jesus' encounter with Peter signals a potential criticism on Mark's part of a militaristic model of messiahship, there is another approach available; it entails examining the way Mark describes the human career of Jesus. In this particular passage, and indeed throughout Mark 8:27–10:52, Jesus consistently reconfigures what true power entails. While the available Jewish sources from this period show that there was no single way of thinking about the Messiah, these same sources employ the concept of Messiah in a way that envisions a leadership figure of one sort or

---

31. Sanders, *The Historical Figure of Jesus*, 88–89.

32. In Matthew, Mark, and Luke, Jesus answers, "You say so" (Matt. 27:11; Mark 15:2; Luke 23:3). In John's Gospel, Jesus answers, "Do you ask this on your own, or did others tell you about me?" (John 18:34).

33. See Craig A. Evans, "King Jesus and His Ambassadors: Empire and Luke-Acts," in *Empire in the New Testament*, ed. Stanley E. Porter and Cynthia Long Westfall, McMaster New Testament Studies (Eugene, OR: Pickwick, 2011), 120–25.

another. One need not be, however, either a military or political fig-ure to wield power. The fact is that most positions of leadership carry within them the temptation to use the position to serve self at the expense of others. Peter clearly does not want his friend and leader to die; more than that, however, Peter's attitude suggests that he con-ceives of leadership the way human beings usually tend to think of it, as an opportunity for prestige, power, and the authority to direct the lives of others for the sake of personal benefit. This is the kind of leader Peter apparently wants Jesus to be. Perhaps this is the kind of leadership to which most people aspire, or at least find tempting. It certainly seems to be the model of leadership most familiar in mod-ern culture. For Mark's Jesus, however, authentic leadership entails attending to the interests of others and serving others. This is the job description, so to speak, for the anointed agent of God who embod-ies God's kingdom:

> So Jesus called them and said to them, "You know that among the Gentiles those whom they recognize as their leaders lord it over them, and their great ones are tyrants over them. But it is not so among you; but whoever wishes to become great among you must be your servant, and who-ever wishes to be first among you must be slave of all. For the Son of Man came not to be served but to serve, and to give his life a ransom for many. (Mark 10:42–45)

This passage highlights two features of the Markan portrait of Jesus: first, Jesus' commitment to live and, if need be, to die as a particular kind of leader, namely, a servant leader, and second, the necessity for the disciples to model their common life after Jesus' life. In view here, then, is a model for a certain way of liv-ing or common life. As Gustavo Gutiérrez notes, "What prompted Peter's objection was his reluctance to accept the consequences of acknowledging that Jesus is the Christ."[34] Jesus is upfront with his disciples that living a life that is committed to serving others is not only rare, but is inevitably open to the reality of suffering and even death: "He called the crowd with his disciples, and said to them,

---

34. Gustavo Gutiérrez, *We Drink from Our Own Wells: The Spiritual Journey of a People*, trans. Matthew J. O'Connell (Maryknoll, NY: Orbis, 1984), 50.

'If any want to become my followers, let them deny themselves and take up their cross and follow me" (Mark 8:34). Taken out of context, this passage can be over-spiritualized to mean that a follower of Jesus should strive to live a life of self-renunciation. Such a reading, however, misses the real point of the summons, which has everything to do with Jesus' command to the disciples to focus not within but on something larger than themselves. As Elizabeth Struthers Malbon notes, crosses were not spiritualized in the first century CE. They were all too real instruments of violent execution that were reserved for persons who were regarded as having challenged those with legitimate power.[35] The larger point that Jesus is making, then, is that a life of commitment to serving others frequently leads to suffering, a fate which history has so often demonstrated to be the case.

The historical figure who perhaps understood this passage best was Martin Luther King Jr. On the eve of his assassination, in his last public speech delivered in the Mason Temple Church of God in Memphis, Tennessee, King concluded his famous mountain top speech with the following words:

> Well, I don't know what will happen now. We've got some difficult days ahead. But it really doesn't matter with me now, because I've been to the mountaintop. And I don't mind. Like anybody, I would like to live a long life. Longevity has its place. But I'm not concerned about that now. I just want to do God's will. And He's allowed me to go up to the mountain. And I've looked over. And I've seen the Promised Land. I may not get there with you. But I want you to know tonight, that we, as a people, will get to the promised land! And so I'm happy, tonight. I'm not worried about anything. I'm not fearing any man! Mine eyes have seen the glory of the coming of the Lord![36]

King was assassinated the following day, April 4, 1968. In a manner reminiscent of the scene where Jesus predicts his own

---

35. Malbon, *Hearing Mark*, 59–62.

36. Martin Luther King Jr., *Testament of Hope: The Essential Writings of Martin Luther King, Jr.*, ed. James M. Washington (San Francisco: Harper, 1986), 286.

In this April 3, 1968 photo, Martin Luther King Jr. delivers his famous "I've Been to the Mountaintop" speech at the Mason Temple in Memphis, Tennessee. On the following day King would be assassinated on the balcony of the Lorraine Motel, now the site of the National Civil Rights Museum.

suffering fate, King reflects on his future with what appears to be a strong premonition concerning his death. At the same time, it is important to note that King emphatically states his preference to continue living. In other words, King was not looking to die. In the same way, Jesus is not looking to die in the narrative of Mark's Gospel. King goes on to say that his focus remains on something larger than himself, something that he describes as the overwhelming commitment to embody or enact God's will in the face of potentially lethal opposition. For Martin Luther King Jr., the embodying or enactment of God's will coincided with the modern civil rights movement and prevailed over his natural human desire for self-preservation. Indeed, King's life hope was to foster the development of what he called "the beloved community," a community guided by a conception of power ruled by love.[37] It would be a mistake to say, however, that King, or Jesus for that matter, was destined to die. Rather, in the course of living out what they discerned to be the will of God, both figures died in keeping with the self-sacrificial character of their lives. As Mark describes it, Jesus challenges the disciples to define their common life

---

37. See Jaroslav Pelikan, *Jesus through the Centuries: His Place in the History of Culture* (New York: Harper, 1985), 217.

no less radically by being prepared to endure resistance for the Gospel message of serving others, whatever the cost. Mark's invitation to his audience is that they be prepared to do the same.

Summary

The religious experience articulated in the Gospel of Mark is marked by deep attentiveness to the significance of the suffering and death of Jesus. Jesus appears in Mark's Gospel as the anointed agent of God who embodies the kingdom, not only through acts of physical and social healing, but above all through his commitment to lead a life that serves others. By means of a highly creative handling of traditions, Mark guides the reader to recognize the suffering and death of Jesus as the decisive events through which to view the public ministry of Jesus. This emphasis receives its fullest and most dramatic expression in the scene of Peter's encounter with Jesus over the question of Jesus' identity as the Messiah. Mark uses this moment in the narrative both to redefine the kind of power that characterizes Jesus' status as Messiah and to reflect on the implications of that power for the shape of common life. Mark had highlighted in earlier episodes of the narrative the a-familial character of the community forming around Jesus. Building on these earlier scenes, Mark employs the encounter between Jesus and Peter to challenge his audience to transform their outlook and behavior in accordance with a new understanding of power, different from the understanding to which they were accustomed. In this we see Mark's role as a shaper of common life.

Questions for Review

1. What are some specific places in Mark's Gospel where the creative ability of the author is most apparent?
2. How does the scene in which Peter identifies Jesus as the Messiah contribute to Mark's understanding of the common life?
3. What are some of the defining features of Mark's portrayal of the disciples?

Questions for Reflection

1. How might the presentation of Jesus in the Gospel of Mark challenge the way notions of power and leadership are typically understood in modern American culture?

2. How does the model for common life proposed in the Gospel of Mark challenge contemporary ways of thinking about community?

3. Why should an appreciation for the essential Jewishness of Jesus be an important requirement for any contemporary interpretation of Mark's Gospel?

For Further Reading

Craig A. Evans, "King Jesus and His Ambassadors: Empire and Luke-Acts." In *Empire in the New Testament*, edited by Stanley E. Porter and Cynthia Long Westfall, 120–39. McMaster New Testament Studies. Eugene, OR: Pickwick, 2011.

Donahue, John R., SJ, and Daniel J. Harrington, SJ. *The Gospel of Mark*. Edited by Daniel J. Harrington, SJ. Sacra Pagina 2. Collegeville, MN: Liturgical Press, 2002.

Gutiérrez, Gustavo. *We Drink from Our Own Wells: The Spiritual Journey of a People*. Translated by Matthew J. O'Connell. Maryknoll, NY: Orbis, 1984.

Hooker, Morna D. *The Gospel According to Saint Mark*. Black's New Testament Commentaries. Peabody, MA: Hendrickson, 1997.

Johnson, Luke Timothy. *The Writings of the New Testament: An Interpretation*. 3rd ed. Minneapolis: Fortress, 2010

King, Martin Luther, Jr. *Testament of Hope: The Essential Writings of Martin Luther King, Jr.*, Edited by James M. Washington. San Francisco: Harper, 1986.

Levine, Amy Jill. *Short Stories by Jesus: The Enigmatic Parables of a Controversial Rabbi*. New York: Harper One, 2014.

Malbon, Elizabeth Struthers. *Hearing Mark: A Listener's Guide*. Harrisburg, PA: Trinity, 2002.

Moloney, Francis J. *The Gospel of Mark: A Commentary*. Peabody, MA: Hendrickson, 2002.

Pelikan, Jaroslav. *Jesus through the Centuries.* New York: Harper, 1985.

Powell, Mark Allan. *Introducing the New Testament: A Historical, Literary, and Theological Survey.* Grand Rapids: Eerdmans, 2009.

Sanders, E. P. *The Historical Figure of Jesus.* New York: Penguin, 1993.

Schröter, Jens. "The Gospel of Mark." In *The Blackwell Companion to the New Testament,* edited by David E. Aune, 272–95. Chichester, UK; London; Malden, MA: Wiley Blackwell, 2010.

Segal, Alan F. *Rebecca's Children: Judaism and Christianity in the Roman World.* Cambridge, MA: Harvard University Press, 1986.

Encountering Matthew

Jesus as Teacher of Living in the Kingdom of Heaven

The previous chapter asserted that the Gospel of Mark served as the principal source for the Gospel of Matthew. If Mark's Gospel appeared sometime around the year 70 CE, and allowing adequate time for its geographical spread, a date within the range of the eighties to nineties CE is a reasonable estimate for the appearance of Matthew.[1]

Placing the Gospel of Matthew in Historical Context

Signs of communal tension in parts of Matthew's Gospel also point to composition during the period soon after the fall of the Temple in Jerusalem. As already noted, at the time when the texts of the New Testament were being written Christianity as a religious movement distinct from Judaism still lay in the future. Even the term Judaism itself is something of a misnomer, since numerous Jewish groups with competing beliefs and practices made up the Jewish political and religious landscape in the first

---

1. Dennis C. Duling, "The Gospel of Matthew," in *The Blackwell Companion to the New Testament*, ed. David E. Aune (Chichester, UK; London; Malden, MA: Wiley Blackwell, 2010), 298.

century.[2] Nevertheless, the period during which Matthew's Gospel emerged witnessed Jews who confessed Jesus to be the Messiah striving to articulate their relationship with fellow Jews who did not share their exalted claims about Jesus. Traces of what amounts to

an intra-familial conflict between different groups of Jews are found throughout Matthew's Gospel. Some of these instances of conflict are quite subtle, as in the scene where the author depicts King Herod and all of Jerusalem as filled with anxiety at the birth of Jesus, the prophesied King of the Jews (Matt. 2:3), or when the author has Jesus refer to Jewish places of prayer and study as "their synagogues" (4:23; 9:35; 10:17; 12:9; 13:54).[3] The latter serves as a clear example of what sociologists might call the use of "othering" language; that is, language that aims to legitimate the claims and status of one group at the expense of another.[4] Other polemical exchanges between Jesus and other Jewish religious groups occur throughout the narra-

Imagery from Ezekiel's vision of four "living creatures" before God's throne (Ezek. 1:5-11) was taken up in Christian iconography to represent the Four Gospels, as in this eleventh-century ivory plaque. The creature resembling a human being is associated with Matthew's Gospel, and also represents Jesus' humanity.

tive.[5] Particularly acrimonious is Matthew 23, in which Jesus vilifies the Pharisees and scribes. The intensity of these disputes—in addition to the fact that the Pharisees seem to have been accorded great status by ordinary Jews—suggests that something more than unbiased historical reminiscence of the ministry of Jesus is at work in these

---

2. The four main groups mentioned in the Jewish literary sources were: the Pharisees, the Sadducees, the Essenes, and the Zealots. For a concise description of these groups and their beliefs, see Maria Pascuzzi, *Paul: Windows on His Thought and World* (Winona, MN: Anselm Academic, 2014), 13–18.

3. See Duling, "The Gospel of Matthew," 305.

4. See also Matt. 27:25.

5. See Donald Senior, CP, "Directions in Matthean Studies," in *The Gospel of Matthew in Current Study: Studies in Memory of William G. Thompson, SJ*, ed. David E. Aune (Grand Rapids: Eerdmans, 2001), 11–12.

episodes. Behind these encounters are glimpses of an ancient audience of Jews laboring hard to defend their new religious commitments and to grow into their own identity as a separate Jewish sect within the already variegated Judaism of the period.

Narrative Artistry in Matthew

One of the most notable structural features of Matthew's Gospel is seen in the five major speeches that Jesus gives throughout the narrative (Matt. 5:1–7:29; 10:1–42; 13:1–58; 18:1–35; 24:1–25:46). Complementing this pattern of five discourses is a more basic organizational structure that divides the Gospel into three major sections signaled by variations on the phrase "From that time Jesus began" (4:17; 16:21).[6] These instances of arrangement are motivated as much by thematic concerns as by the author's attention to matters of literary symmetry. By alternating speech and narrative sections in the narrative, Matthew encourages the audience to work out for themselves the precise relationship between the ministry of Jesus as a teacher with other aspects of Jesus' public ministry, such as his work as a healer and exorcist.

The Narrative Flow of Matthew

First Division (1:1–4:16)
Defining the Origins of Jesus, God's Obedient Son
Ancestral genealogy of Jesus; angelic announcement of Jesus' conception by God's Spirit; events associated with the birth of Jesus; preaching of John concerning repentance; the baptism of Jesus; the testing in the wilderness.

Second Division (4:17–16:20)
Public Ministry of Teaching and Healing among the People of Israel
Call of the first disciples; summary statement of healings; the Sermon on the Mount; stories of healings, controversies

Continued

---

6. Luke Timothy Johnson, *The Writings of the New Testament: An Interpretation*, 3rd ed. (Minneapolis: Fortress, 2010), 167.

with religious leaders, and the first sea miracle; commissioning and sending out of the Twelve to proclaim the gospel and heal; Jesus' public ministry among Israel and further controversies with religious leaders; the parables; rejection at Nazareth; death of John the Baptist; feeding of the 5,000 and second miracle at sea; more controversies with religious leaders, second feeding story (4,000), Peter's confession.

Third Division (16:21–28:20)
The Suffering and Vindication of God's Son

Predictions concerning Jesus' death and vindication, lessons on discipleship, the transfiguration of Jesus; extended teaching on behavior expected of members of the church; counter-cultural teachings, final stories of healing, scenes of misunderstanding on the part of the disciples, final prediction concerning suffering and death; arrival in Jerusalem, disturbance in the Temple, confrontations and controversies with religious leaders and Temple elites, parables of judgment; denunciation of scribes and Pharisees and lament over Jerusalem; prediction of fall of the Temple, teachings and parables on the need for watchfulness; scene of final judgment of the world; narration of the events of Jesus' last days, death by crucifixion, burial, and guard placed at tomb; account of the empty tomb and appearances of resurrected Jesus, final commission of Jesus to disciples.

Jesus as Teacher: Preliminary Observations on Common Life and Religious Experience

The previous chapter maintained that Matthew creatively adapted Mark, in part by supplementing him with a more extensive body of teaching material. While all four Gospels preserve the memory that Jesus was a teacher, the Gospel of Matthew has traditionally been called "the teacher's Gospel" due to the prominence of the activity of teaching in its presentation of the public ministry of Jesus.[7] Matthew portrays Jesus as a challenging and, at times, even an unsettling teacher.[8] There is little evidence from Matthew to corroborate the popular Hollywood-movie depiction of a Jesus whose instruction consists of timeless moral truths or bland spiritual principles.[9] Instead, Matthew depicts a figure who frequently confronts his audience with uncomfortable truths.

For example, like many of the Jewish prophets before him, Jesus consistently confers honor on the poor and vulnerable (Matt. 5:3–5) while at the same time criticizing the rich. In fact, Jesus has positively alarming things to say to those who prioritize wealth in their lives: "Do not store up for yourselves treasures on earth, where moth and rust consume and where thieves break in and steal; but store up for yourselves treasures in heaven, where neither moth nor rust consumes and where thieves do not break in and steal. For where your treasure is, there your heart will be also" (6:19–21). And a bit further on in the same chapter, Matthew's Jesus declares, "No one can serve two masters; for a slave will either hate the one and love the other, or be devoted to the one and despise the other. You cannot serve God and wealth" (6:24; see also 19:16–26). None of these teachings are comforting to hear; it is much easier to neglect the poor or rationalize poverty as a choice. Jesus also advocates priorities that prove extremely demanding to live out in any consistent sort of manner.

---

7. See W. D. Davies, *The Sermon on the Mount* (Cambridge, UK: Cambridge University Press, 1966), 129–31. See also Morna D. Hooker, *Beginnings: Keys that Open the Gospels* (Harrisburg, PA: Trinity, 1997), 25.

8. See Amy Jill Levine, *Short Stories by Jesus: The Enigmatic Parables of a Controversial Rabbi* (New York: HarperOne, 2014), 23.

9. A notable exception here would be Pier Paolo Pasolini's 1964 film, *The Gospel of Matthew*. The following is an excerpt from the late Roger Ebert's review of the film focusing on the film's depiction of Jesus: "His personal style is sometimes gentle, as during the Sermon on the Mount, but more often he speaks with a righteous anger, like a union organizer or a war protester. His debating style, true to Matthew, is to answer a question with a question, a parable, or dismissive scorn. His words are clearly a radical rebuke of his society, its materialism, and the way it values the rich and powerful over the weak and poor. No one who listens to this Jesus could confuse him for a defender of prosperity, although many of his followers have believed he rewards them with affluence." Roger Ebert, "The Gospel According to St. Matthew," Great Movie, Roger Ebert.com, *https://www.rogerebert.com/reviews/great-movie-gospel-according-to-st-matthew-1964*.

Dietrich Bonhoeffer

One example of a modern figure who seems to have compre-
hended the radical nature of Jesus' priorities was the Lutheran

theologian Dietrich Bon-
hoeffer, whom the Nazis ex-
ecuted on April 9, 1945, for
his part in a plot to assas-
sinate Adolph Hitler. In his
influential book *The Cost
of Discipleship*, Bonhoeffer describes the vocation
demanded of the authen-
tic disciple of Jesus in this
way: "When Christ calls a
man, he bids him come and
die."[10] Although the death
envisioned by Bonhoeffer
certainly involves the possibility of physical death,
it also points to a pattern
of living that Bonhoeffer
characterizes elsewhere as
"costly," precisely because
it requires of the disciple a
life of counter-cultural difference from the standards

A statue of Lutheran minister Dietrich Bonhoeffer stands in the west
façade of Westminster Abbey. Bonhoeffer believed it to be his Christian duty to resist the Nazi regime;
he paid for his convictions with his
life on April 9, 1945.

of the surrounding culture.[11] The cost of such a pattern of living inevitably entails the loss of personal status and, in some
cases, even one's life.

The demanding nature of the common life envisioned by Jesus
is perhaps nowhere more evident than in chapter 18 of the Gospel,

---

10. Dietrich Bonhoeffer, *The Cost of Discipleship*, trans. R. H. Fuller (New York:
Touchstone, 1995), 89.

11. Bohoeffer, *The Cost of Discipleship*, 45.

where alone among the Synoptic Gospels the Greek word *ekklēsia* ("assembly" or "church") is applied to the community of Jesus' followers.[12] Earlier it was noted that the term "assembly" or "church" referred in the ancient world to the civic body of a region's citizenry. In ancient Greece and Rome, the citizen body constituted the embodied public space in which elite males could compete against one another for the purpose of gaining an honorable reputation. In accordance with this model of citizenship or common life the acquisition of social distinction, what we might define as *greatness*, was understood to be the result of rising above one's peers. A far different standard of *greatness* is put on display in this section of Matthew:

> At that time the disciples came to Jesus and asked, "Who is the greatest in the kingdom of heaven?" He called a child, whom he put among them, and said, "Truly I tell you, unless you change and become like children, you will never enter the kingdom of heaven. Whoever becomes humble like this child is the greatest in the kingdom of heaven. Whoever welcomes one such child in my name welcomes me." (Matt. 18:1–5)

In a passage that Matthew has selectively copied from Mark, the privileged members of the citizen body of the kingdom of heaven are depicted as children and greatness is measured, not in terms of rising above others, but in serving others in humility. Moreover, those singled out as the special recipients of service are depicted as children. Much of the remainder of the chapter focuses on the behavior to be accorded to those members of the church community described as "little ones," a description that likely refers to those members of the community who lacked social power and influence. Jesus warns the more powerfully placed members of the church not to cause offense to "these little ones" or to "despise . . . these little ones" (Matt. 18:6, 10). Note the personal tone of these warnings, especially the latter admonition that reckons so honestly with the toxic emotion of scorn. With this warning, Jesus indicts the all too frequent inclination to devolve into communal dysfunction through attitudes and behaviors

---

12. The word appears a total of three times in Matthew: once in 16:18 in reference to Peter, and twice in 18:17.

that signal contempt for others, in particular those who have less social capital, whether due to cultural, economic, or gender status. The moral seriousness of the issue is highlighted by the use of exaggerated and violent language: it is better to sever a hand or foot, or pluck out an eye, than to cause offense (18:8–9). Here Jesus employs metaphors for thinking imaginatively, if somewhat grotesquely, of certain dimensions of the human personality, namely, the way people choose to treat others (hands and feet) and the way people choose to view or regard others (eye).[13] The metaphorical dismemberment points to the painful transformation of attitude and behavior that, while in keeping with the values of the kingdom, is at the same time at odds with the way human beings typically behave in fellowship with each other. This call to a selfless form of common life focused on the benefit of the *little ones* serves as the foundation for the broader admonition found near the end of the discourse, where the importance of forgiveness and reconciliation within the "church" comes into view. In the fellowship of members with one another, the church is to cultivate a common life that embodies a contrast to the frightening ease with which human beings dismiss and exploit others for their own advantage.

The teaching of Jesus in Matthew's Gospel also stands out for its emphasis on concrete praxis or behavior. For example, near the conclusion of the Sermon on the Mount, Jesus warns, "Not everyone who says to me, 'Lord, Lord,' will enter the kingdom of heaven, but only the one who does the will of my Father in heaven" (Matt. 7:21). In this passage Jesus envisions entrance into the kingdom as conditional upon behavior that accords with the will of God; mere faith in Jesus is not enough. A similar perspective appears in the parable of the Sheep and the Goats (25:31–46). In that parable, unique to Matthew's Gospel, compassionate acts of social justice directed to the marginalized constitute the necessary behavior that alone merits the reward of salvation in the age to come: "Then the king will say to those at his right hand, 'Come, you that are blessed by my Father, inherit the kingdom prepared for you from the foundation of the world; for I was hungry and you gave me food, I was thirsty and you gave me something

---

13. See Bruce J. Malina and Richard L. Rohrbaugh, *Social-Science Commentary on the Synoptic Gospels*, 2nd ed. (Minneapolis: Fortress, 2003), 419–20.

to drink, I was a stranger and you welcomed me, I was naked and you gave me clothing, I was sick and you took care of me, I was in prison and you visited me" (25:34–36). Nowhere in this parable is faith per se even mentioned; what is of consequence to Jesus are embodied acts of compassion that relieve instances of tangible suffering.

Finally, Matthew's understanding of Jesus as a challenging and counter-cultural teacher is also shaped by the early Christian faith commitment in the resurrection of Jesus.[14] Sharing with his audience the religious experience that Jesus is alive and powerfully present to the community, Matthew's distinctive adaptation of this experience is to depict Jesus as a very special kind of teacher, one who transcends the Gospel narrative and addresses the audience directly as a powerful, living presence.[15] Consequently, the teachings of Jesus function for Matthew's audience as much more than simply articulations from the past; they function most essentially as exhortations to the community by the risen Jesus to live transformed lives in the present.[16]

The Sermon on the Mount and the Values of the Kingdom of Heaven

The remainder of this chapter will focus on the first of the five speeches given by Jesus in the Gospel of Matthew: the Sermon on the Mount (5:1–7:29). There are two reasons for this focus. First, in addition to being the longest of the five speeches, the Sermon on the Mount functions as the inaugural event of Matthew's Gospel. As the speech that contains the first public words delivered by Jesus, the sermon functions to delineate the essential features of the character of Jesus and foreshadows important themes that will recur in later parts of the narrative. In other words, the Sermon on the Mount can

---

14. Already in Paul's letters, the earliest documents in the New Testament, the conviction that Jesus was raised from the dead to new life is described as normative and established tradition: "For I handed on to you as of first importance what I in turn had received: that Christ died for our sins in accordance with the scriptures, and that he was buried, and that he was raised on the third day in accordance with the scriptures" (1 Cor. 15:3–4).

15. Jack Dean Kingsbury, *Matthew as Story*, 2nd ed. (Philadelphia: Fortress, 1988), 107–13.

16. See Ulrich Luz, *Studies in Matthew* (Grand Rapids: Eerdmans, 2004), 23.

be regarded as programmatic for the remainder of Matthew's Gospel. Second, while it would be incorrect to argue that the themes of religious experience and common life are restricted to this particular section of the Gospel, it is equally the case that these themes are especially prominent in the Sermon on the Mount.

Much of the content of Matthew's Sermon on the Mount also appears in the Gospel of Luke.[17] In contrast to Matthew, who prefers to organize his material into thematic clusters, Luke places this material in a number of different locations in his Gospel (Luke 6:20–34; 9:51–18:15). While it is possible that Jesus gave multiple speeches or even reused material in different situations, a more likely scenario is that the two evangelists have made their own creative decisions on how to order this material in accordance with their distinctive thematic purposes.[18] The sermon begins in a manner that is immediately evocative of the theme of common life: Jesus is seated on a mountain surrounded by his disciples. As numerous scholars attentive to the dynamics of effective storytelling have observed, settings in the Gospels frequently overflow their surface meaning and evoke an assortment of symbolic associations.[19] In this instance, the specification of a mountain functions to recall the scriptural account of the giving of the Law to Moses on Mount Sinai (Exod. 19–24), as well as the concept of divine revelation more generally (see Exod. 19:18; 34:5). The mountain setting also points forward to the story of the transfiguration of Jesus (Matt. 17:1–8) and the appearance of the risen Jesus (Matt. 28:16–20). In the former, three of the disciples experience a visionary foretaste of the glory that Jesus will receive at his resurrection accompanied by a divine voice identifying Jesus as God's Son (Matt. 17:5). In the latter, the resurrected Jesus

---

17. The presence of a high level of verbal agreement in this material suggests that Matthew and Luke also had access to another written source that they used to supplement Mark. This source, which scholars call Q, from the German word *Quelle* ("source"), appears to have been a collection of mostly sayings of Jesus. The fact that an independent copy of Q has never been found may be a testament to the skill with which both Matthew and Luke incorporated its contents into a larger narrative framework, rendering Q obsolete as a separate document.

18. Frank J. Matera, *The Sermon on the Mount: The Perfect Measure of the Christian Life* (Collegeville, MN: Liturgical Press, 2013), 7–9.

19. Kingsbury, *Matthew as Story*, 28. See also David Rhoads, *Reading Mark: Engaging the Gospel* (Minneapolis: Fortress, 2014), 13–14.

commissions the disciples to teach the nations and assures them of his continued presence among them. The reader is reminded once again that Jesus is a unique kind of teacher, for he is also the risen Lord of the community. For this reason, the disciples depicted in the opening lines of the sermon serve to include the contemporary audience for whom Matthew is writing his Gospel.[20] Integral to the shared religious experience of this community is the conviction that the risen Jesus directly addresses them in the present just as the human Jesus addressed the gathered disciples in the past.

This last observation has particular relevance for the theme of common life in Matthew and accounts for the distinction Matthew makes between two audiences for the sermon. While the "crowds," as Matthew calls them, overhear the sermon (see Matt. 7:28), these are essentially a secondary audience whose members are free to choose whether to commit themselves to Jesus or not. As the remainder of the Gospel shows, most do not. The disciples, however, have already made an initial commitment to follow Jesus;[21] as the primary recipients of Jesus' teaching, they are summoned to put the teachings of Jesus into tangible form.[22]

Living Out Now the Future Kingdom of Heaven

The sermon proper begins with an introduction that extends through the first sixteen verses of chapter 5. The centerpiece of this section are the eight blessings (or "beatitudes") in which Jesus blesses particular classes of persons as well as the behaviors and attitudes that identify them.[23]

---

20. Kingsbury, *Matthew as Story*, 107–9.

21. To be precise, thus far in the narrative Jesus is presented as having called only four disciples: Simon, Andrew, James, and John. This peculiarity underscores just how closely Matthew adheres to the overall outline of Mark's Gospel even when this presents an inconsistency in the narrative.

22. See Bonhoeffer, *The Cost of Discipleship*, 105–6; see also Matera, *The Sermon on the Mount*, 29.

23. Some count nine beatitudes. However, the use of the second person plural, "you," in 5:11, as opposed to the recurring use of the third person plural in the first eight beatitudes, suggests that the choice of eight is probably correct. See Ulrich Luz, *Matthew 1–7: A Critical and Historical Commentary on the Bible*, Hermeneia (Minneapolis: Fortress, 2007), 185.

> Blessed are the poor in spirit, for theirs is the kingdom
> of heaven.
>
> Blessed are those who mourn, for they will be comforted.
>
> Blessed are the meek, for they will inherit the earth.
>
> Blessed are those who hunger and thirst for righteousness,
> for they will be filled.
>
> Blessed are the merciful, for they will receive mercy.
>
> Blessed are the pure in heart, for they will see God.
>
> Blessed are the peacemakers, for they will be called children
> of God.
>
> Blessed are those who are persecuted for righteousness' sake,
> for theirs is the kingdom of heaven. (Matt. 5:3–10)

The blessing formula that recurs throughout this list is not unique to Jesus. It is used in the Jewish Scriptures to designate the honorable status of a faithful Jew who places complete trust in the God of Israel and who looks to the Jewish Law or Torah as the place to discern the will of God (see Ps. 1:1; Prov. 8:32–34).[24] Despite the link between faithfulness and Torah observance, it would be a mistake to understand the Beatitudes as an assortment of rules.[25] Their true import becomes clearer only when they are connected to the theme of the kingdom of heaven, a reality that Matthew understands to be dawning with the appearance of Jesus on the public stage: "Jesus went throughout Galilee, teaching in their synagogues and proclaiming the good news of the kingdom and curing every disease and every sickness among the people" (Matt. 4:23).

As already discussed, the concept of the kingdom of heaven or the kingdom of God is creatively ambiguous. When thought of as a spatial and temporal concept, it refers generally to a place—either in heaven or more typically on earth—where God's rule will be exercised in the age to come.[26] At the same time, the concept has

---

24. While the Hebrew term *Torah* can be translated as "law," "guidance" or "instruction" are also appropriate translations.

25. See Matera, *The Sermon on the Mount*, 27.

26. The sense of the kingdom as a physical location is also present in Matthew: "Truly I tell you, at the renewal of all things, when the Son of Man is seated on the throne of his glory, you who have followed me will also sit on twelve thrones, judging the twelve tribes of Israel" (Matt. 19:28).

a strongly experiential quality in the sense that it expresses a way of being and acting in the world that conforms to what God values. References to the kingdom appear in the first and eighth beatitudes: "Blessed are the poor in spirit, for theirs is the kingdom of heaven" (Matt. 5:3) and "Blessed are those who are persecuted for righteousness' sake, for theirs is the kingdom of heaven" (5:10). This example of literary framing encourages the reader to view the Beatitudes as illustrating important aspects of the nature of the kingdom.

Perhaps the most striking feature of the blessings involves the surprising makeup of the groups whom Jesus calls blessed. These are not the kinds of persons who generally receive honor in society, either then or now. Jesus' generally negative attitude toward wealth has already been noted. Just as counter-intuitive—though not, of course, from the perspective of the Jewish Scriptures—is the opening blessing pronounced on the poor in spirit (Matt. 5:3). Since certain passages in the Gospel suggest that there were persons of wealth in Matthew's community (see 10:9), it is sometimes suggested that, in deference to these wealthy members of the congregation, Matthew tries to interiorize Jesus' blessings. It is argued that this tendency becomes most apparent once Matthew's beatitudes are compared to Luke's more concise list (Luke 6:20–22). Whereas Matthew's poor and hungry could possibly be understood figuratively, Luke unambiguously refers to the literally poor and hungry.[27] Others, such as Bonhoeffer, note that Matthew's Jesus is in fact speaking of the literally poor: "Privation is the lot of the disciples in every sphere of their lives. . . . They have no security, no possessions to call their own, no earthly society to claim their absolute allegiance. . . . For his sake they have lost all."[28] The last part of this quote, in particular the phrase, "For his sake," is important to consider. Poverty is not something that should be glamorized or romanticized as a desirable or higher state of being. What makes the poor disciples blessed is not the state of deprivation itself. Rather, their blessedness lies in a commitment to follow Jesus in response to his call, despite the cost to their lives that such following will likely entail.

The inclination to interiorize the beatitudes, however, is not entirely unjustified, since the blessings also highlight specific

---

27. See Johnson, *The Writings of the New Testament*, 177.

28. Bonhoeffer, *The Cost of Discipleship*, 107.

attitudes or sensibilities that shape particular ways of relating to God and behaving in the world. Poverty of spirit, for example, envisages an attitude of complete dependence upon God, while the blessing bestowed upon the peacemakers (Matt. 5:9) speaks to a commitment to cultivate reconciliation. The blessing on the meek (5:5) imparts praise to those who do not assert their power over others, while the blessing on the merciful (5:7) prioritizes compassion as the defining ethic for social interaction with other human beings. This particular blessing also complements a defining characteristic of the God of Israel. In the book of Exodus, the Lord descends upon Mount Sinai in a cloud and proclaims to Moses, "The LORD, the LORD, a God merciful and gracious, slow to anger, and abounding in steadfast love and faithfulness" (Exod. 34:6). The implication is that such attitudes and behaviors reflect something of the very character of God.

This religious experience of transcendence together with the translation of such experience into behavior helps to clarify the relationship between the kingdom of heaven and the virtues expressed in the Beatitudes. In a total of six of the eight blessings, the reward that the blessed receive is clearly oriented toward the future: "they will be comforted" (Matt. 5:4), "they will inherit the earth" (5:5), "they will be filled" (5:6), "they will receive mercy" (5:7), "they will see God" (5:8), "they will be called children of God" (5:9). On the one hand, this emphasis on future reward functions to direct our attention away from the groups who received blessing to a transcendent reality, namely, the kingdom of heaven, a reality which ultimately is a gift given by God in the age to come. The New Testament scholar Frank Matera points out, "Their blessedness or happiness, then, is not so much the result of their own effort as it is the result of the gift of final salvation that God brings with the kingdom."[29] On the other hand, the temporal emphasis on the future also speaks to the observation born of experience that the persons and qualities envisioned in the Beatitudes are rare in the world.

In so far as the attitudes and behaviors expressed in the blessings reveal something of the transcendent character of God, they

---

29. Matera, *The Sermon on the Mount*, 31.

also give expression to what we might characterize as the values of the kingdom. Although the kingdom is fundamentally a future reality, the disciples are invited at the start of the sermon to live their lives in accordance with these values in the present. There is a real challenge here: although the kingdom is ultimately a gift, the disciples are nonetheless called to behave in certain ways in order to gain entrance into the kingdom. How they behave matters, even more than what they believe: "Not everyone who says to me, 'Lord, Lord,' will enter the kingdom of heaven, but only the one who does the will of my Father in heaven" (Matt. 7:21). Fortunately for the disciples, the present experience of the power of the kingdom allows for the possibility of a personal transformation in the present that will only be fully perfected in the age to come. Put another way, the future gift of the kingdom empowers and summons the disciples to live in a fundamentally new way.

Common Life and the Pedagogy of the Kingdom of Heaven

The theme most on display in the lengthy middle section of the Sermon on the Mount (Matt. 5:17–7:12) concerns what the shape of a life lived in light of the values of the in-breaking kingdom looks like. Twice employing the phrase, "the law and the prophets," first in 5:17 and then again in 7:12, Matthew signals to the reader that the material framed by these two literary brackets should be read as unit. The application of this framing technique illustrates one of Matthew's chief purposes in this part of the sermon, which is to depict Jesus as a teacher who reveals the deeper meaning of Torah.

The principal topic of Jesus' instruction throughout the section relates to the concept of righteousness: "For I tell you, unless your righteousness exceeds that of the scribes and Pharisees, you will never enter the kingdom of heaven" (Matt. 5:20). The concept of righteousness derives from the symbolic world of the Jewish Scriptures. Righteousness is, above all, a relational concept that is related closely to the covenant consciousness of the Jewish people. While there did not exist in the Second Temple period anything like what one might call a uniform Judaism, certain core convictions were shared by all Jews, convictions that constituted what E. P. Sanders has termed "Common Judaism."[30] Among these convictions was a belief in divine election, namely, the belief that God had chosen to enter into a special relationship with the Jewish people. Jews believed that God had bestowed uniquely on them the Law or Torah, which functioned to govern and guide every aspect of a Jew's life.[31] Once one recognizes this link between the concepts of righteousness and covenant, it becomes clear that righteousness had everything to do with being in right relationship or good standing with God. Since it was believed, moreover, that the revealed will of God was located in Torah, it followed that the way to cultivate this right relationship was to observe the precepts of Torah. Attendant upon the experience of being in right relationship with God was the confidence that one was at peace with God in the present and could look forward to the gift of the kingdom in the age to come. This does not mean, however, that first-century Jews thought that divine approval could be earned by Torah observance. Jews observed Torah as part of their commitment both to honor God and to keep alive their lived experience of intimate relationship with God.[32] Only by viewing the concept of righteousness with such relational ideas in mind can one understand how first-century Jews conceptualized what they were doing when they observed the precepts of Torah.

Since it was understood that righteousness has everything to do with the observance of Torah, it is not surprising that the interpretation of Torah comprises a significant feature of the teaching of Jesus in this section of the sermon. Beginning in 5:21 and extending through 5:48 are six sayings of Jesus that are sometimes misleadingly characterized as the Antitheses. In these statements Jesus first quotes a passage from Torah and then proceeds to give his own authoritative interpretation of it. As Frank Matera points out, the description of these six sayings as antithetical in character is a misnomer, since Jesus

---

30. E. P. Sanders, *The Historical Figure of Jesus* (London: Penguin, 1993), 33–34. The Second Temple period extended roughly from 519 BCE to 70 CE. The period begins with the rebuilding of the Temple in Jerusalem (in 519 BCE) after its destruction by the Babylonian Empire in 586 BCE and ends with the destruction of the second Temple in 70 CE during the Jewish War against Rome.

31. Sanders, *The Historical Figure of Jesus*, 37.

32. See E. P. Sanders, *Paul and Palestinian Judaism: A Comparison of Patterns of Religion* (Minneapolis: Fortress, 1977), 85–125.

never presents his teaching as in any way opposed to Torah.[33] If anything, Jesus' teachings function as an extension of Torah. That is, for both Matthew and his audience the teachings function as windows for glimpsing the deeper intention of the will of God believed to be inscribed in the scriptural text. The goal of each of the six teachings is to illumine for the disciples certain features of a new pattern of common life whose distinguishing feature is the depth of its commitment to righteousness.

The first four teachings pertain to the Torah's prohibition of murder, adultery, divorce, and the swearing of oaths. The final two teachings address, respectively, the interpretation of Torah regarding retaliatory violence and the boundaries of communal commitment. It is sometimes said that these teachings emphasize the need to correlate intention with behavior, but this reading tends to over-prioritize the first two teachings (on murder and adultery); in fact, the majority of the statements say little about matching intention to behavior. The statements do, however, disturb customary patterns of thought and behavior for the purpose of constructing new ways of thinking about and acting in community. Viewed collectively, Jesus' extensions of teachings found in the Torah envision a model of communal fellowship that intensifies the ideal of love of neighbor inscribed in both the Torah and the concluding antithesis in the Sermon on the Mount (Matt. 5:43–48; 19:19). Thus love of neighbor entails being mindful of the potential for angry speech to erode communal fellowship (5:21–26); love of neighbor entails avoiding sexual aggression and exploitation (5:27–32); love of neighbor entails telling the truth (5:33–37). And above all else, love of neighbor, if it is to be perfect, entails giving priority to the practical and often difficult task of reconciliation with others.

An indication of the supreme importance placed by Jesus on the goal of reconciliation is its prioritization in the first antithetical teaching dealing with anger: "So when you are offering your gift at the altar, if you remember that your brother or sister has something against you, leave your gift there before the altar and go; first be reconciled to your brother or sister; and then come and offer your gift" (Matt. 5:23–24). For Jesus, a first-century Jew, the Temple in

---

33. See Matera, *The Sermon on the Mount*, 50.

Jerusalem was believed to be the location where the invisible presence of God dwelled in a unique manner. Jesus effectively places reconciliation with another member within the community on the same level as the worship of God in the Temple. This link between love of God and neighbor—already highly traditional in the Judaism of Jesus' day—becomes explicit later in the narrative in the response of Jesus to a Pharisee who asks him to point to the greatest commandment in Torah: "He said to him, 'You shall love the Lord your God with all your heart, and with all your soul, and with all your mind.' This is the greatest and first commandment. And a second is like it: 'You shall love your neighbor as yourself'" (22:37–39).

Whereas in the teaching concerning anger Jesus addresses circumstances that can lead to the fracturing of fellowship for those who have already committed themselves to living together in community, in the final two teachings he turns to instances where the community experiences outright hostility against its very existence. Jesus calls on the disciples in these instances to embody reconciliation in highly creative ways. In the antithesis focusing on retaliation (Matt. 5:38–42), Jesus quotes a provision from Torah that sought to redress the injustice of victimization by allowing a response that was proportional to the original injustice (Matt. 5:38; cf. Exod. 21:24). Already in Torah there is a move to respond to hostility in a creative way by limiting the natural desire for vengeance. Jesus extends this teaching:

> You have heard that it was said, "An eye for an eye and a tooth for a tooth." But I say to you, Do not resist an evil-doer. But if anyone strikes you on the right cheek, turn the other also; and if anyone wants to sue you and take your coat, give your cloak as well; and if anyone forces you to go one mile, go also the second mile. (Matt. 5:38–41)

When students come across this passage they sometimes ask one of two questions, and even sometimes both. First, is this teaching meant to be taken literally? Second, if we do take it literally, what possibly could be the logic behind it, since experience suggests that perpetrators of violence will usually, if given the chance, take multiple advantage of their victims? As for the first question, Martin Luther King Jr. said of Jesus in his famous sermon on loving one's

A non-violent civil rights protest takes place at a Woolworth lunch counter sit-in in Tallahassee, Florida. The refusal of such protesters to respond to violence with violence embodied Jesus' teaching to "turn the other cheek" (Matt. 5:38-41).

enemies (Nov. 17, 1957), "He wasn't playing."[34] For someone like King, then, retaliation does seem to be prohibited by Jesus in an absolute sense. As for the second question ("What is the logic behind the prohibition of violence?") a potential answer involves the recognition of the deceptively creative power inherent in acts of non-violent resistance. Dietrich Bonhoeffer offers the following insight on the matter: "The only way to overcome evil is to let it run itself to a standstill because it does not find the resistance it is looking for. . . . By refusing to pay back the enemy in his own coin, and by preferring to suffer without resistance, the Christian exhibits the sinfulness of contumely and insult. Violence stands condemned by its failure to evoke counter-violence. When a man unjustly demands that I should give him my coat, I offer him my cloak also, and so counter his demand; when he requires me to go the other mile, I go willingly, and show up his exploitation of

34. Martin Luther King Jr., " 'Loving Your Enemies': Sermon Delivered at Dexter Avenue Baptist Church," in *The Papers of Martin Luther King Jr.*, vol. 4, *Symbol of the Movement: January 1957–December 1958*, ed. Clayborne Carson (Berkeley: University of California Press, 2000), 316.

my service for what it is."[35] It is significant that in this passage Bonhoeffer employs words such as "exhibits" and "shows up." The creative power residing in such acts of non-resistance lies not least in the fact that they reveal in a highly public way the unjust violence of the perpetrator and the alternate road taken by the victim of violence. Witnessing the first spectacle is terrible, while witnessing that of the second is surprising and inspiring. One thinks of that famous picture from the civil rights era of young African-American and white students absorbing the humiliation of having milkshakes poured over their heads at a segregated lunch counter. Their decision not to retaliate constitutes neither an empty gesture nor an impractical rejection of reality. Rather, their non-violent resistance engenders enough of a pause in the cycle of violence to open up the potential for a new way forward.

The concluding teaching on love of enemy draws a universal application from the previous teaching. Of all the teachings, this one is perhaps the strangest instruction in that Jesus appears to make a mistake! Torah does indeed enjoin love of neighbor (Lev. 19:18), but nowhere does the Torah call for hatred of one's enemy. A potential way forward out of this difficulty is to see Jesus acting here as a spokesperson for how the commandment to love is often enacted in the concrete as a way to limit the boundaries of those whom we think deserve our love.[36] How different is God, whose love is universal; the God who sends sunshine and rain upon everyone. The potentially transformative power of this teaching makes sense only when it is understood that Jesus is not speaking here about overcoming hostility with a kind of affection for those who are our enemies. For King, as well as for Jesus, the love here in view is not an emotion, but an active kind of power that takes seriously the presence of evil, but nonetheless seeks to transform it: "And it is significant that he does not say, 'Like your enemy.' Like is a sentimental something, an affectionate something. There are a lot of people that I find difficult to like. I don't like what they do to me. I don't like what they say about me and other people. I don't like their attitudes. I don't like some of the things they're doing. I don't like them. But Jesus

35. Bonhoeffer, *The Cost of Discipleship*, 141–42.

36. Matera, *The Sermon on the Mount*, 62–63.

says love them. And love is greater than like. Love is understanding, redemptive goodwill for all men, so that you love everybody, because God loves them."[37]

King's choice of words in this quote is illuminating; he speaks of love as having a "redemptive goodwill." Later in the same sermon, King similarly links what he calls the "power of redemption" to love of enemies.[38] While King does not make the following explicit, such references to the biblical concept of redemption seem to touch ultimately on what is a transcendent claim, which is that such radically reconciling love conforms to the very nature of God, who "makes his sun rise on the evil and on the good, and sends rain on the righteous and on the unrighteous" (Matt. 5:45). If this assessment is in any way accurate, it may also have a bearing on the way one should interpret Jesus' invitation to the disciples at the end of chapter 5: "Be perfect, therefore, as your heavenly Father is perfect." The perfection that Jesus has in view, therefore, is relational in character. To be perfect does not entail faultlessness, but rather a commitment to a path of embodying a new way of living in community that is ultimately enabled by the experience of one's relationship to God (see 7:7–11).

In the remainder of the Sermon on the Mount, Jesus continues to focus on the theme of righteousness and its implications for renewed common life. In chapter 6 Jesus turns his attention to the three acts of religious devotion whereby first-century Jews both cultivated and demonstrated the love of God commanded of them in Torah (Deut. 6:5): charitable giving, prayer, and fasting. The perfect righteousness that Jesus has in view as it relates to the three acts of piety is in some ways an amplification and explication of the sixth beatitude, "Blessed are the pure in heart, for they will see God" (Matt. 5:8). As Matera observes, purity of heart has everything to do with transparency to the will of God: "The pure in heart are single-minded in their devotion to God. They are not divided or conflicted in their allegiance to God, trying to please both God and human beings. They have only one goal and purpose—to please God, and so their heart is pure because of its undivided allegiance to God."[39] Whether the

---

37. King, "Loving Your Enemies," 319–20.

38. King, "Loving Your Enemies," 321.

39. Matera, *The Sermon on the Mount*, 40.

action is charitable giving, prayer, or fasting, the clear teaching is that self-promotion compromises one's relationship with God.

Once again, Jesus' teaching appears quite disorienting. Viewed in light of the importance placed in ancient society on the public recognition of a person's honor or reputation, the call to forego public approval for the sake of the private and hidden approval of God seems impractical to say the least. These teachings take on additional poignancy when one recalls that members of Matthew's community have probably had to endure occurrences of social persecution from the surrounding culture (see Matt. 5:10–11) with the diminishment of honor that invariably accompanied such marginalization. How psychically painful this must have been! And how tempting it must have been to seek ways to regain lost honor and reputation. Matthew's readers would hear in the words of Jesus an appeal to see their honorable status as residing, instead, in God's approval.

The lengthy middle section of the sermon concludes with Jesus evoking still other scenarios in which the righteousness that is in accord with God's will and the kingdom can be enacted.[40] Not surprisingly there are teachings on the dangers associated with wealth (Matt. 6:19–24); a lesson that focuses on the need for absolute dependence upon God (6:25–34); and teachings on judgment that highlight once again the theme of reconciliation (7:1–5). Interestingly, the list is far from exhaustive, showing that Jesus allows for significant freedom in terms of discerning other ways that one can embody the alternative values of the kingdom.[41] This aspect of freedom also helps to clarify the way the Sermon on the Mount arrives at its conclusion in 7:13–29. Through the use of ordinary and familiar images, such as gates, roads, trees, and houses, Matthew impresses upon his audience the clear warning that the teachings articulated in the sermon are meant not only to be heard, but above all to be embodied in a common life that anticipates in the present the future arrival of the kingdom.

---

40. Kingsbury, *Matthew as Story*, 112.

41. See Ulrich Luz, *The Theology of the Gospel of Matthew* (Cambridge, UK: Cambridge University Press, 1995), 54–55.

Summary

This chapter has examined the role of religious experience and common life in the Gospel According to Matthew through the lens of Jesus as teacher. For Matthew and his audience, the teachings of Jesus transcend the historical memory of his words and are experienced as ways to encounter the resurrected presence of Jesus. In the teachings of the Sermon on the Mount, Matthew's audience hears the voice of one whom they experience as alive in a new way and receives instruction into a new model of communal fellowship. The alternative values inscribed in the Sermon on the Mount both interrogate and disorient ingrained cultural assumptions and behaviors by envisioning a common life empowered by the very different values of the kingdom of heaven.

Questions for Review

1. How should one define the concept of perfection encountered in the Sermon on the Mount?
2. What significance does belief in the resurrection of Jesus play in Matthew's understanding of Jesus as a teacher?
3. How would you describe the character of the teaching of Jesus encountered in the Sermon on the Mount?
4. What does the concept of righteousness refer to in the Gospel of Matthew?

Questions for Reflection

1. What groups in contemporary culture could be associated with the Beatitudes?
2. What specific teachings from the Sermon on the Mount might prove helpful in thinking about issues of common life in contemporary culture?
3. Many contemporary Christians claim that Jesus prioritized faith over against works. Does the Sermon on the Mount support or contradict this view? How does it do so?

For Further Reading

Bonhoeffer, Dietrich. *The Cost of Discipleship*. Translated by R. H. Fuller. New York: Touchstone, 1995.

Davies, W. D. *The Sermon on the Mount*. Cambridge, UK: Cambridge University Press,1966.

Duling, Dennis C. "The Gospel of Matthew." In *The Blackwell Companion to the New Testament*, edited by David E. Aune, 296–318. Chichester, UK; London; Malden, MA: Wiley Blackwell, 2010.

———. *The Gospel of Matthew in Current Study: Studies in Memory of William G. Thompson, SJ*. Grand Rapids: Eerdmans, 2001.

Hartin, Patrick J. *Exploring the Spirituality of the Gospels*. Collegeville, MN: Liturgical Press, 2010.

Hooker, Morna D. *Beginnings: Keys That Open the Gospels*. Harrisburg, PA: Trinity, 1997.

Johnson, Luke T. *The Writings of the New Testament: An Interpretation*. 3rd ed. Minneapolis: Fortress, 2010.

King, Martin Luther, Jr. "'Loving Your Enemies': Sermon Delivered at Dexter Avenue Baptist Church." In *The Papers of Martin Luther King Jr*. Vol. 4, *Symbol of the Movement: January 1957–December 1958*, edited by Clayborne Carson, 316. Berkeley: University of California Press, 2000.

Kingsbury, Jack Dean. *Matthew as Story*. 2nd ed., revised and enlarged. Philadelphia: Fortress, 1988.

Levine, Amy Jill. *Short Stories by Jesus: The Enigmatic Parables of a Controversial Rabbi*. New York: HarperOne, 2014.

Luz, Ulrich. *Matthew 1–7*. Edited by Helmut Koester. Translated by James E. Crouch. Hermeneia. Minneapolis: Fortress, 2007.

———. *Studies in Matthew*. Translated by Rosemary Selle. Grand Rapids: Eerdmans, 2005.

———. *The Theology of the Gospel of Matthew*. Translated by J. Bradford Robinson. Cambridge, UK: Cambridge University Press, 1995.

Malina, Bruce J., and Richard L. Rohrbaugh. *Social-Science Commentary on the Synoptic Gospels*. 2nd ed. Minneapolis: Fortress, 2003.

Matera, Frank J. *The Sermon on the Mount: The Perfect Measure of the Christian Life.* Collegeville, MN: Liturgical Press, 2013.

Pascuzzi, Marie. *Paul: Windows on His Thought and World.* Winona, MN: Anselm Academic, 2014.

Rhoads, David, Joanna Dewey, and Donald Michie. *Mark as Story: An Introduction to the Narrative of a Gospel.* 2nd ed. Minneapolis: Fortress, 1999.

Sanders, E. P. *The Historical Figure of Jesus.* New York: Penguin, 1993.

———. *Paul and Palestinian Judaism: A Comparison of Patterns of Religion.* Minneapolis: Fortress, 1977.

Senior, Donald., CP. "Directions in Matthean Studies." In *The Gospel of Matthew in Current Study: Studies in Memory of William G. Thompson, SJ,* edited by David E. Aune, 5–21. Grand Rapids: Eerdmans, 2001.

4

Encountering Luke

The Journey of Faith in Community

O ne of the most distinctive writings found in the New Testament is the Gospel of Luke, sometimes also known as the Third Gospel. Even in the ancient world, many viewed this Gospel and the writing called the Acts of the Apostles as together representing a unified work written by the same author.[1] The two texts share notable verbal and thematic similarities, including a preface addressed to an otherwise unknown "Theophilus," the apparent patron of both volumes.[2] If correct, this consensus permits one to perceive in Luke-Acts the earliest unified narrative account of not only the life, death, and resurrection of Jesus (Luke's Gospel) but also the history of the early church down to Luke's own generation (the book of Acts).[3]

The Purpose of Luke's Gospel and Its Literary Achievement

What might have motivated the author to compose such a work? Scholarly judgments differ on this question and it is quite probable

---

1. Richard P. Thompson, "Luke-Acts: The Gospel of Luke and the Acts of the Apostles," in *The Blackwell Companion to the New Testament*, ed. David E. Aune (Chichester, UK; London; Malden, MA: Wiley Blackwell, 2010), 319.

2. Thompson, "Luke-Acts," 319. See Luke 1:1–4; Acts 1:1–5.

3. It is important to note that not all scholars agree that Luke-Acts is a unity. See Patricia Walters, *The Assumed Authorial Unity of Luke and Acts: A Reassessment of the Evidence* (Cambridge, UK: Cambridge University Press, 2009).

that no single reason accounts fully for the origin of Luke's ambitious two-volume project. An argument could be made, however, that by Luke's day the social makeup of early Christianity may have contributed in some way to the need for a text such as Luke-Acts. Near the end of the first century, the majority of Luke's readers would have identified both ethnically and religiously as Gentile or non-Jewish.[4] That is, they neither would have traced their lineage back to the people of Israel, nor would they have necessarily lived like Jews in accordance with Jewish Torah observance.[5] As a consequence, many among Luke's audience—even its Jewish Christian members—might have been curious about the process whereby a small movement comprised exclusively of Jews centered in the city of Jerusalem came to find its most receptive hearing from a predominantly non-Jewish audience residing in the major urban centers of the Greco-Roman world. Perhaps aware of such curiosity, the author of Luke-

The Metropolitan Museum of Art, Gift of J. Pierpont Morgan, 1917

Imagery from Ezekiel's vision of four "living creatures" before God's throne (Ezek. 1:5-11) was taken up in Christian iconography to represent the Four Gospels, as in this eleventh-century ivory plaque. The creature resembling an ox is associated with Luke's Gospel, and also represents Jesus' embracing the role of a servant.

Acts accounts for this rather surprising outcome of events by grounding the roots of the development of the Christian movement in both the Jewish Scriptures and the providential guidance of the God of Israel.[6]

The most stylistically sophisticated of the four New Testament Gospels, the Third Gospel opens with an introductory

4. While most scholars would likely place the composition of Luke-Acts sometime near the end of the first century, there are good reasons to consider a date in the early second century. See Richard Pervo, *Dating Acts: Between the Evangelists and the Apologists* (Santa Rosa, CA: Polebridge, 2006).

5. Thomas H. Tobin, SJ, *The Spirituality of Paul* (Eugene, OR: Wipf & Stock, 1987), 80–81.

6. See Thompson, "Luke-Acts," 327. See also John T. Carroll, *Luke: A Commentary* (Louisville: Westminster John Knox, 2012), 5, and W. C. van Unnik, "Luke-Acts: A Storm Center in Contemporary Scholarship," in *Studies in Luke-Acts*, ed. Leander E. Keck and J. Louis Martyn (Nashville: Abingdon, 1966), 25.

preface that may provide yet another clue concerning the motivations of the author:

> Since many have undertaken to set down an orderly account of the events that have been fulfilled among us, just as they were handed on to us by those who from the beginning were eyewitnesses and servants of the word, I too decided, after investigating everything carefully from the very first, to write an orderly account for you, most excellent Theophilus, so that you may know the truth concerning the things about which you have been instructed. (Luke 1:1–4)

The first lines of Luke's Gospel would have made a positive impression on educated readers in the ancient world who were familiar with the highly stylized manner in which historical writings of the period began.[7] For example, included in Luke's preface are references to previous sources as well as the testimony of past eyewitnesses, details that immediately would have been recognized as key elements of the genre of ancient historiography.[8] As a result of his investigations, Luke promises to provide his patron with a narrative that is carefully arranged, persuasive, and expressive of the "truth" (Luke 1:4). It is worth noting that the Greek underlying this noun might just as well be translated as "security," implying that Luke seeks to assure his patron, as well as other auditors, that the faith that now defines their lives has not been misplaced.[9] Luke's patron might also have detected in the preface a prominent communal tone as signaled both by Luke's reference to the "many" who have preceded him in compiling narratives about Jesus and the mention of the memory of events passed down to "us." Such expressions evocative of communal gathering serve to assure Luke's audience that the story he is about to tell takes its beginning from a community of shared commitments and continues to be articulated anew by the present community to which the author and his audience belong.

---

7. Pheme Perkins, *Introduction to the Synoptic Gospels* (Grand Rapids: Eerdmans, 2007), 213. See also, Joel B. Green, *The Theology of the Gospel of Luke* (Cambridge, UK: Cambridge University Press, 1995), 17–18.

8. François Bovon, *Luke 1: A Commentary on the Gospel of Luke 1:1–9:50*, trans. Christine M. Thomas, Hermeneia (Minneapolis: Fortress, 2002), 5.

9. See Morna D. Hooker, *Beginnings: Keys That Open the Gospels* (Harrisburg, PA: Trinity, 1997), 46.

The Narrative Flow of Luke

First Division (1:5-4:13)
The Birth of Jesus and Salvation for Israel
Prologue to Luke's Gospel; angelic announcement of the births of John the Baptist and Jesus; births of Jesus and John the Baptist; scenes in the Temple, appearance of John in the wilderness; baptism of Jesus followed by his genealogy; testing of Jesus in the wilderness.

Second Division (4:14-9:50)
Jesus the Prophet in Action
Inaugural sermon in Nazareth; stories of healings and exorcisms; confrontations with religious leaders; stories centering on the disciples; predictions of suffering and death.

Third Division (9:51-19:27)
Teaching on the Way to Jerusalem
Teaching lessons for the disciples; final stories of healing; warnings to the crowds; confrontations with religious leaders; predictions of suffering and death.

Fourth Division (19:28-24:53)
Rejection and Vindication of God's Son
Arrival in Jerusalem; teaching in the Temple; more confrontations with religious leaders; Jesus' final days (arrest, execution); empty tomb and resurrection appearance stories.

Religious Experience, Common Life, and Legitimation in Luke's Birth Story

Philip Esler employs the sociological concept of legitimation in an effort to clarify the purpose of Luke-Acts.[10] As defined by Esler, the category of legitimation refers to the various beliefs and practices

---

10. Philip Frances Esler, *Community and Gospel in Luke-Acts: The Social and Political Implications of Lucan Theology* (Cambridge, UK: Cambridge University Press, 1987), 16.

that a community points to in an attempt to justify its existence to its own membership.[11] Specifically, the task of legitimation entails the construction of a conceptually coherent account of the origins of a new communal grouping. For the members of a new community who had previously identified with competing cultural and religious traditions, the work of legitimation, when pursued successfully, promotes the psychological assurance and confidence needed to sustain a new way of life.[12]

Luke was writing for a group still in its early stages of existence, a community of mostly first- and second-generation Christians that found itself surrounded by already established and thriving Greco-Roman and Jewish communities.[13] Living in an ancient culture whose inhabitants both revered what was ancient and looked with suspicion on anything considered recent or novel, many of the first Christians undoubtedly struggled over issues of identity owing to the relative newness of their community. Faced with such challenges, many of these early Christians would have felt the need to clarify for themselves the precise nature of their common life. Luke's Gospel was written, at least in part, for just such an audience that was eager to define their past and anticipate their future.

The Religious Experience of Jesus' Unique Origins in God in the Birth Narrative

Luke begins his engagement with issues of communal identity in the context of his narration of the events associated with the conception and birth of Jesus. Clustered throughout this section

---

11. Esler, *Community and Gospel in Luke-Acts*, 16–17. Luke Timothy Johnson notes that the "purpose" of Luke-Acts "is to interpret the Gospel for insiders within the context of a pluralistic environment composed of both Jews and Gentiles." See Luke Timothy Johnson, *The Gospel of Luke*, ed. Daniel J. Harrington, SJ, Sacra Pagina 3 (Collegeville, MN: Liturgical Press, 1991), 9.

12. Esler, *Community and Gospel in Luke-Acts*, 17.

13. In order to appreciate better the marginality of these primitive communities one only needs to recall that the total number of Christians by the late first century was likely around several thousand. See Marcus J. Borg and John Dominic Crossan, *The First Paul: Reclaiming the Radical Visionary Behind the Church's Conservative Icon* (New York: HarperOne, 2009), 90.

The Metropolitan Museum of Art, Robert Lehman Collection, 1975

Fifteenth-century artist Botticelli depicts the angel Gabriel announcing to Mary that she will conceive God's Son through the agency of the Holy Spirit, represented by the faint rays of light radiating from behind the angel.

of the narrative are a number of highly honorific claims regarding Jesus. Luke in particular highlights the royal status of Jesus, as in the scene where Mary, Jesus' mother, is visited by the angel Gabriel: "And now, you will conceive in your womb and bear a son, and you will name him Jesus. He will be great, and will be called the Son of the Most High, and the Lord God will give to him the throne of his ancestor David. He will reign over the house of Jacob forever, and of his kingdom there will be no end" (Luke 1:31–33). The royal status of Jesus is again in view in the scene where shepherds receive a revelation of the angel of the Lord: "But the angel said to them, "Do not be afraid; for see—I am bringing you good news of great joy for all the people: to you is born this day in the city of David a Savior, who is the Messiah, the Lord" (2:10–11). Both passages likely are intended to evoke for Luke's readers the prophecy found in 2 Samuel 7:12–16. In that passage, God promises King David, through the agency of the prophet Nathan, that he will establish David's kingdom forever and honor as his son one of David's descendants: "I will raise up your offspring after you, who shall come forth from your body, and I will establish his kingdom. He shall build a house for my name, and I will establish the throne of his kingdom forever. I will be a father to him, and he shall be a son to me" (2 Sam. 7:12–14).[14] References to the motif of the royal status of Jesus appear elsewhere in the infancy narrative as well (see Luke 1:69; 2:4).

While establishing the royal identity of Jesus is important to Luke, what counts as the highest honorific claim made about Jesus in the birth account involves Luke's understanding of the ultimate origins of Jesus. Although Luke, like Matthew, considers Joseph to be an adoptive father to Jesus, Luke will claim that the origins of Jesus rest uniquely in God by virtue of the conception of Jesus by God's Spirit: "The angel said to her, "The Holy Spirit will come upon you, and the power of the Most High will overshadow you; therefore the child to be born will be holy; he will be called Son of God" (Luke 1:35). What might Luke have meant by this?

Perhaps for many contemporary Christians the language of "Spirit" or "Holy Spirit" calls to mind the classical Christian doctrine of the Trinity, of which the Holy Spirit is the Third Person.[15] But it is important to recognize that this precise formulation arose centuries after the New Testament was written. While an argument can be made that the basis of the doctrine of the Trinity can be traced back to scriptural warrants, it must also be recognized that these same scriptural warrants only imperfectly and imprecisely complement later theological formulations.[16] The original matrix for the concept of spirit is, in fact, a Jewish one. As employed in the Jewish Scriptures, spirit designates not a person, but the creative power of God (see Ezek. 36:27; 37:14; Zech. 12:10), especially as that power is manifested and experienced in some new and dramatic way. Important to mention here are the numerous sources

---

14. Even if Luke's audience was largely comprised of Gentiles such implicit references to the Jewish Scriptures would not necessarily be foreign to them. Esler makes the important observation that at least some among Luke's audience were "God-fearers." These were Gentiles who were not full converts to Judaism but had attended synagogue. Since the synagogue was a place where the Jewish Scriptures was studied, they could have recognized these references, even if left implicit. See Esler, *Community and Gospel in Luke-Acts*, 24–45.

15. See Jaroslav Pelikan, *Jesus through the Centuries: His Place in the History of Culture* (New York: Harper & Row, 1985), 57–70.

16. See Raymond E. Brown, *Responses to 101 Questions on the Bible* (New York: Paulist Press, 1990), 25.

from the Jewish Scriptures that looked to a future day when the God of Israel would bestow the spirit upon the covenant people in a fuller and more glorious fashion. The biblical book of Joel offers a classic formulation of this expectation: "Then afterward I will pour out my spirit on all flesh; your sons and your daughters shall prophecy, your old men shall dream dreams, and your young men shall see visions. Even on the male and female slaves, in those days, I will pour out my spirit" (Joel 2:28–29; see also Acts 2:16–17). If one thinks of the phrases "God's spirit" or the "Holy Spirit" as ways that the Jewish Scriptures talk about the presence of God, it becomes clearer why so many texts in the New Testament associate the disclosure of God's presence with the life-giving event of Jesus' resurrection from the dead (see, e.g., Acts 2:29–36; John 20:22). Reflecting on the ultimate origins of Jesus in light of this more traditional affirmation concerning the resurrection of the adult Jesus, Luke takes a step backwards and locates his audience's experience of the life-giving presence of God at the earliest stage of the human career of Jesus, at the very moment of his conception by the Spirit. The conviction that the divine presence uniquely abides in Jesus and is the ultimate source of his origin functions as the highest honor claim made about Jesus in Luke's birth account.

Common Life and Salvation as Liberation in the Birth Narrative

In what way, however, might these considerations relate to the topic of common life? To begin to answer that question, it might be helpful to attend to the characters who appear in Luke's birth account. Introduced first are the figures of Elizabeth and Zechariah (Luke 1:5–25), the first of a total of three male and female paired couples encountered in the story. The others are Mary and Joseph, the parents of Jesus, and Simeon and Anna, who together are closely associated with the Temple in Jerusalem. The parents of John the Baptist are defined—as indeed are all the major Jewish characters in the birth story (see 2:22–25, 36–38, 41–42)—by their piety: "Both of them were righteous before God, living blamelessly according to all the commandments and regulations of the Lord" (1:6). This in conjunction with their significant age (1:7) and their priestly pedigree

(1:5) single them out as highly honorable figures in a culture that glorified advanced age and took matters of religious observance and lineage seriously. However, Zechariah and Elizabeth are confronted with the obstacle of infertility (1:7, 25, 57–58), a severe hardship, especially for Elizabeth (1:25). This circumstance speaks less to any marks of marginality in either Zechariah or Elizabeth than it does to the reality that disappointment visits everyone, including the religiously observant.

Luke's audience would have associated the characters of Zechariah and Elizabeth with the scriptural figures of Abraham and Sarah who, as a consequence of their significant age, also faced the inability to have a child (Gen. 18:11–15). Just as God made it possible for Abraham and Sarah to conceive, so Zechariah and Elizabeth experience the deeply personal joy and relief (Luke 1:13–14) that results from receiving at last the gift of a hoped-for child. Luke paints an image of the God of Israel as a loving God who brings tangible joy and fulfillment into the lives of God's people (see Luke 1:14, 30, 47–49, 58; 2:10).

Throughout the remainder of the birth account, Luke continues to emphasize this theme of fulfillment. For example, Mary rejoices that she has been favored by God to receive the unexpected gift of conceiving the child who will be heir to King David's throne as well as Son of God (Luke 1:46–55). Simeon lives to see the fulfillment of the vision granted by the Holy Spirit that he would see the Messiah before his death (2:25–32). And the aged widow Anna pauses in prayer to praise God for the gift of redemption embodied in the child Jesus (2:36–38).

These passages help account for why Luke takes such evident care to describe both the God of Israel and Jesus as Savior figures. Luke is, by far, the evangelist who speaks the most often about salvation.[17] Twice in Luke's infancy narrative the term *Savior* appears as a description of God and Jesus, respectively (Luke 1:47; 2:11), while two forms of the noun *salvation* occur a total of four times (1:69, 71, 77; 2:30). The basic definition of a Savior in the Greco-Roman period was that of a human being or a deity who gave concrete aid or deliverance to persons in distress. In the Jewish

---

17. Green, *The Theology of the Gospel of Luke*, 94; Johnson, *The Gospel of Luke*, 23.

Scriptures, particularly in the Psalms, the concept of salvation is linked especially to the historic acts of physical deliverance of the Jewish people by the God of Israel (see 1:69–74). Similarly, the joy and fulfillment experienced by Zechariah and Elizabeth is a matter of embodied fulfillment: salvation in the form of a gift of an unexpected child. This theme of salvation as embodied fulfillment first announced in the infancy narrative continues to be emphasized in the remainder of the Gospel through the many stories of how Jesus relieves people from the bondage of physical suffering and demonic possession.

At the same time, the birth of John the Baptist holds a larger significance for the common life of the Jewish people: "But the angel said to him, "Do not be afraid, Zechariah, for your prayer has been heard. Your wife Elizabeth will bear you a son, and you will name him John. You will have joy and gladness, and many will rejoice at his birth, for he will be great in the sight of the Lord. . . . Even before his birth he will be filled with the Holy Spirit. He will turn many of the people of Israel to the Lord their God" (Luke 1:13–16). This passage concerning the destiny of John the Baptist contains the first occurrence of the phrase "Holy Spirit" in the birth account (1:15). Here it functions not as a way of speaking about the unique origins of Jesus as discussed above, but as an announcement of a new act by God through which the community of the covenant, the Jewish people, will be renewed and made ready for their long anticipated salvation (1:68–75). By virtue of being both filled with and guided by the Spirit, John will be an essential instrument of this new act of salvation, but only as one preparing the way for the one conceived by the Spirit, Jesus (1:76).

It might be useful to pause here and appreciate the sensitivity with which Luke addresses the lived experience of his audience through these stories. Consider the story of Simeon. Simeon's prediction concerning a response of opposition to Jesus (Luke 2:34–35) may well mirror disagreements and uncertainties about the significance of Jesus in Luke's own community. Is Jesus, as Anna believes, the one in whom the redemption of Jerusalem would be realized (2:38)? Has Jesus truly inherited the throne of his ancestor David as well as a kingdom that will never end (1:32–33)? Such questions were likely on the minds of many of Luke's readers, however committed they may have been. Why else, after all, did Luke promise his patron in the prologue that his Gospel narrative would provide him with a narrative that was secure (1:4)?

Luke would have his readers understand that in the very midst of this new creative activity of a loving God are echoes of previous divine acts of visitation for the salvation of the covenant community. In other words, Luke sees within these more recent events associated with the beginnings of the Christian community the replication of a pattern of God's past manifestations of salvific presence on behalf of the Jewish people. Even Mary's celebration of the most creative act of all, the conception of Jesus by God's Spirit (1:35), recalls the scriptural account of the joy of Hannah when she learns that she will give birth to Israel's first prophet, Samuel (1 Sam. 1:26–2:10). Luke's readers are being led to understand that while their foundational story is new, it is not a novelty unconnected to the noble heritage of previous revelations of God's liberating presence. Indeed, the very unfolding of these events on the world stage of Roman and Jewish politics testifies to their far from obscure significance. For Luke's readers, who perhaps found themselves uncertain of their new status as a result of their transformed religious commitments, the infancy narrative serves to link their new and undoubtedly challenging experience of common life with the scriptural record of God's involvement in Israel's past. They are being encouraged to understand that their story is simultaneously old as well as unexpectedly new.

On the Way with Jesus

A careful reading of the Third Gospel reveals that Luke, like Matthew, took over many of the stories from Mark, while at the same time creatively adapting them in the process. Signs of such creativity are especially evident in the lengthy middle section of the Gospel (Luke 9:51–19:27). In this segment of the narrative, Luke omits many of the stories found in the central section of Mark's Gospel and replaces them with episodes either unique to Luke or in some cases shared with Matthew. Such careful editing results in a significant expansion of the account of Jesus' journey to Jerusalem found in Mark 8:22–10:52 into an extensive ten-chapter journey narrative in Luke.[18] Throughout this section of the Gospel, Jesus is depicted by Luke as a prophetic spokesperson for God. That is, like the Jewish prophets before him, Jesus is tasked with the vocation to reveal and model for the people of God the kinds of behavior and attitudes that accord with the values of God and God's kingdom. In terms of the organizational structure of this part of Luke's Gospel, the following observations might be made: First, in contrast to the material that precedes it, this section of the Gospel places much greater emphasis on the teaching activity of Jesus than on his miracles. Second, a clear geographical concern animates this portion of the narrative as the author depicts Jesus making his way gradually to the city of Jerusalem.[19] Hence, the frequent scholarly designation of this section of the Gospel as the Lukan journey or travel narrative.[20]

Luke has Jesus address several different kinds of audiences throughout the course of the journey narrative, including the disciples, the crowds, and the religious authorities.[21] Of these three distinct groups, the disciples appear the most often and receive the most instruction from Jesus. In conjunction with the narrative device of a lengthy journey to the city of Jerusalem, this focus on the disciples lends a strong tone of identity formation to this entire section of the Gospel. The journey commences with Luke stating that Jesus and the disciples "were going along the road" (Luke 9:57). On one level, the reference to the "road" functions simply as a geographical indicator as well as a reminder to the reader that a physical journey has begun. On a deeper level, however, the "road"—which can just as easily be translated as the "path" or "way"—has clear vocational implications. Such an association was already available in the Jewish Scriptures, where one finds the language of two ways being used to depict in a metaphorical fashion a life of fidelity to God in contrast to a life

---

18. Patrick, J. Hartin, *Exploring the Spirituality of the Gospels* (Collegeville, MN: Liturgical Press, 2010), 45.

19. Green, *The Theology of the Gospel of Luke*, 102–5.

20. Patrick Hartin points out that the journey motif would have been readily familiar to ancient readers from stories found both in the Jewish Scriptures and narratives from the larger Greco-Roman world, such as Homer's *Illiad* and *Odyssey* and Virgil's *Aeneid*. See Hartin, *Exploring the Spirituality of the Gospels*, 48–49.

21. Johnson, *The Gospel of Luke*, 164–65.

of disobedience (see Deut. 11:26–32). What will be the way of life that the disciples will embody as emissaries of Jesus entrusted with the proclamation of the kingdom of God? By the time Jesus has "set his face to go to Jerusalem" (Luke 9:51), the disciples have already encountered in numerous ways the signs of the presence of the kingdom embodied in Jesus' ministry (Luke 11:20). Jesus now invites the disciples through his teaching in the journey narrative to translate their experience of the dawning rule of God into a transformed way of living and behaving with one another and in the world.

The journey narrative is filled with a rich variety of teaching lessons. Some have to do with stories that point out how the poor have less because the rich have more (Luke 16:13, 19–31; 18:18–25).[22] Others encourage the counter-cultural behavior of serving others and cultivating solidarity with the powerless (14:7–14). Still others celebrate the inclusion of women (10:38–42; 13:10–17; 18:2–8; cf. 7:11–17; 8:1–3). Viewed collectively, the various teaching lessons function as reminders to the disciples that theirs is to be a common life characterized by counter-cultural ways of thinking and patterns of behaviors.

Throughout the Gospel of Luke, and in particular within the journey narrative, Jesus is depicted as someone who places extraordinary value on human relationships and who is attuned to the obstacles that complicate or imperil interpersonal relationships. Some of these impediments to common life are no doubt familiar from our own experience. We tend not to want to associate, perhaps with some justification, with those whom we consider to be deviant (Luke 5:27–32). Who cannot relate to the annoyance of a character like Martha who complains to Jesus about her sister, Mary, who sits at the feet of Jesus while Martha attends to the household chores (10:38–42)? And whether one happens to have siblings or not, the story of a dysfunctional family (15:11–32) wracked by envy, jealousy, and irresponsible parenting, is forever relatable. Centering as they do on the theme of strained or even fractured relationships, stories such as these provoke readers to reckon honestly with, and to reexamine,

---

22. See the discussion of issues of economics in the area of ethics in Amanda C. Miller, "Bridge Work and Seating Charts: A Study of Luke's Ethics of Wealth, Poverty, and Reversal," *Interpretation* 68, no. 4 (2014): 416–27.

their assumptions about the nature of common life and the importance of reconciliation. The remainder of this chapter will take up the exploration of these topics through an examination of two parables that are unique to Luke's Gospel: The parable of the rich man and Lazarus (16:19–31) and the parable of the Samaritan (10:29–37).

The Parable of the Rich Man and Lazarus

There was a rich man who was dressed in purple and fine linen and who feasted sumptuously every day. And at his gate lay a poor man named Lazarus, covered with sores, who longed to satisfy his hunger with what fell from the rich man's table; even the dogs would come and lick his sores. The poor man died and was carried away by the angels to be with Abraham. The rich man also died and was buried. In Hades, where he was being tormented, he looked up and saw Abraham far away with Lazarus by his side. He called out, "Father Abraham, have mercy on me, and send Lazarus to dip the tip of his finger in water and cool my tongue; for I am in agony in these flames." But Abraham said, "Child, remember that during your lifetime you received your good things, and Lazarus in like manner evil things; but now he is comforted here, and you are in agony. Besides all this, between you and us a great chasm has been fixed, so that those who might want to pass from here to you cannot do so, and no one can cross from there to us." He said, "Then, father, I beg you to send him to my father's house—for I have five brothers—that he may warn them, so that they will not also come into this place of torment." Abraham replied, "They have Moses and the prophets; they should listen to them." He said, "No, father Abraham; but if someone goes to them from the dead, they will repent." He said to him, "If they do not listen to Moses and the prophets, neither will they be convinced even if someone rises from the dead." (Luke 16:19–31)

The story of the rich man and Lazarus is, in one sense, a story that centers on the theme of a reversal of fortunes. Addressing

This stained-glass window from St. Mary Abbot's Church on Kensington High Street, London, portrays the rich man and Lazarus (Luke 16:19-31). By depicting the two figures in close proximity, the artist hints at a detail in Luke's story: the rich man knows Lazarus by name.

the rich man, the character of Father Abraham—remembered frequently in the Jewish tradition as a paragon of hospitality—says, "Child, remember that during your lifetime you received your good things, and Lazarus in like manner evil things; but now he is comforted here, and you are in agony"(16:25). Indeed, the story emphasizes what we might call the theme of salvation as reversal. That is, instances of deliverance or rescue in the sense of a profound reversal of status whereby those who presently find themselves powerless and marginalized experience empowerment and fulfillment in their lives.[23] This emphasis on the theme of salvation as reversal is one reason why Luke's Gospel is prized among scholars of liberation theology. As defined by Gustavo Gutiérrez, liberation theology concerns itself with theological reflection that is attentive to the lived experiences of those who find themselves excluded, neglected, and frequently exploited by those with power.[24] The character of Lazarus would seem to fit this description nicely.

The preferred method of teaching employed by Luke's Jesus is the use of parables, a teaching style rooted in the Jewish Scriptures.

---

23. Green, *The Theology of the Gospel of Luke*, 94.

24. Gustavo Gutiérrez, *We Drink from Our Own Wells: The Spiritual Journey of a People*, trans. Matthew J. O'Connell (MaryKnoll, NY: Orbis, 1984), 1–2.

Defined literally, the word *parable* means to place something next to or alongside something else for the purpose of constructing a comparison. As noted by Amy Jill-Levine, the parables operate on listeners by provoking them to reflect on familiar matters in new or even disorienting ways.[25] For this reason, Levine proposes that we think less about what a parable might mean and give more attention to what a parable does.[26] This particular parable certainly raises some difficult questions. For example, although the rich man represents what today we might call the fabulously affluent, while Lazarus represents the poorest of the poor, it is curious that are we not given any information about the quality of the moral life of either of the characters. In particular, why was Lazarus carried away by the angels to enjoy a comfortable afterlife? Was it simply because he was poor? If so, does not this romanticize poverty and send a terrible message that poverty is somehow not an evil but a blessing? As for the rich man, what precisely is his sin, so to speak, for which he is suffering so terribly in the afterlife? Is the possession of money and goods itself depicted as evil? Or does the fault of the rich person lie somewhere else? Finally, what lessons about common life does Luke want his readers to take away from this parable?

We live, of course, in a society where affluence and economic acquisitiveness are celebrated as worthy goals. The parable begins by depicting an extreme example of someone who has attained these goals. He dresses in designer clothing and eats lavishly every day (Luke 16:19). We do not so much encounter a simple correlation between wealth and sin as we do an implicit invitation to readers to examine their priorities. Is such prosperity, while undoubtedly comfortable, the purpose of life? And a question more alarming still, does wealth on the scale described in the parable lead inevitably to a callous disregard for everyone else, in particular the Lazaruses of the world?

A focus on common life seems especially clear in the scene in the afterlife where familial language abounds. Seemingly oblivious to why he is in torment, the rich man asks Father Abraham to compel Lazarus to serve him and make his circumstances a bit more comfortable. The rich man—whom we now discover knows Lazarus by

---

25. Amy-Jill Levine, *Short Stories by Jesus* (New York: HarperOne, 2014), 4–5.

26. Levine, *Short Stories by Jesus*, 4.

name—essentially views Lazarus as a slave. His failure to see any solidarity between himself and Lazarus is further underscored by his rather selfish request to save the necks of his brothers: "Then, father, I beg you to send him to my father's house—for I have five brothers—that he may warn them, so that they will not also come into this place of torment" (Luke 16:27–28). In a final rebuff to the rich man, Father Abraham responds that these will not receive any more revelation than what is already in the Jewish Scriptures, where care for the poor is a consistent theme (16:29).

The sin of the wealthy man—a sin of which he never repents—resides in his failure to see any cords of solidarity and common life with someone less fortunate than himself. As a result of this omission he loses the gift of salvation. The stakes turn out to be quite high indeed. The counter image of the rich man in this parable would appear to be the chief tax collector Zacchaeus, whom we encounter a few chapters later (Luke 19:1–10). He also is described as rich, but as a result of his decision both to divest himself of half of his possessions and to make even more than the required restitution to the poor he is assured of nothing less than salvation (19:8–9). Unlike the wealthy man in the parable, Zacchaeus does repent. His salvation lies in embracing in a concrete, embodied way his shared common life with the poor.

The Parable of the Samaritan

The parable of the Samaritan also explores the topic of reconciliation and relationships. This popular story appears only in Luke's Gospel, near the beginning of the journey narrative in a chapter devoted almost exclusively to the topic of missionary outreach (see Luke 10:1–23). A lawyer approaches Jesus with the intention of testing him and seeks his opinion on the kinds of behavior that, if performed, would enable one to inherit eternal life (10:25). Jesus turns the question on the lawyer and asks, "What is written in the law? What do you read there?" The lawyer then responds by quoting what are in fact two separate passages from the Jewish Scriptures (Deut. 6:5 and Lev. 19:18) that were frequently linked by pious Jews as a single commandment that summed up the entirety of the Torah: "You shall love the Lord your God with all your heart, and with all your soul, and with all your strength, and with all your mind; and your neighbor as yourself" (Luke

In this icon of the Parable of the Samaritan by Giovani Paulo Bardini, Chiesa di San Pietro, Bologna, three figures pass by the wounded traveler, but only one, the Samaritan, fulfills the biblical command, "Love your neighbor."

10:27).[27] Satisfied by this answer, Jesus affirms the Lawyer's response and encourages him to live out such a love of God and neighbor in the concrete details of his own life (Luke 10:28).

In commenting on this scene, Amy Jill-Levine notes two ways in which the lawyer depicted by Luke is misguided. First, he works with the erroneous assumption that eternal life can be merited, forgetting that it is in fact a gift. Second, while his instinct that eternal life has a deep connection with behavior is correct, he wrongly concludes that a single, one-time action is required and nothing more.[28] Unhappy with Jesus' open-ended response, the lawyer presses Jesus into clarifying who in fact his neighbor is. This request leads directly into the parable:

> But wanting to justify himself, he asked Jesus, "And who is my neighbor?" Jesus replied, "A man was going down from Jerusalem to Jericho, and fell into the hands of robbers, who

27. The original Hebrew of Deuteronomy lacks the phrase "with all your mind."

28. Levine, *Short Stories by Jesus*, 78.

stripped him, beat him, and went away, leaving him half dead. Now by chance a priest was going down that road; and when he saw him, he passed by on the other side. So likewise a Levite, when he came to the place and saw him, passed by on the other side. But a Samaritan while travelling came near him; and when he saw him, he was moved with pity. He went to him and bandaged his wounds, having poured oil and wine on them. Then he put him on his own animal, brought him to an inn, and took care of him. The next day he took out two denarii, gave them to the innkeeper, and said, 'Take care of him; and when I come back, I will repay you whatever more you spend.' Which of these three, do you think, was a neighbor to the man who fell into the hands of the robbers?" He said, "The one who showed him mercy." Jesus said to him, "Go and do likewise." (Luke 10:29–37)

An appreciation for the historical relations between Samaritans and Jews in antiquity is helpful for understanding this parable. While Samaritans were ethnically related to Jews, their origins lay in the distant past when two rival kingdoms located in the north and south of Roman Judea, respectively, emerged in the wake of the disintegration of the united Jewish kingdom under the Kings David and Solomon in the tenth century BCE. The split was widened further after the northern kingdom of Israel succumbed to invading Assyrian armies in 721 BCE. The Assyrians deported much of the population of the northern kingdom and then proceeded to colonize the area with different ethnic groups.[29]

Samaritans and Jews disagreed over fundamental issues of religious identity. The two groups saw different cities as the true capital of the covenant people of God (Samaria and Jerusalem, respectively), worshipped at different temples, and disagreed over the precise content and interpretation of the Jewish Scriptures. Further resentment was fueled on both sides by periodic acts of violence, most notably the burning down of the temple in Samaria by Jewish forces in 128 BCE. This history of conflict helps to illuminate the scene at the very beginning of the journey narrative (Luke 9:52–56). A certain

---

29. See Levine, *Short Stories by Jesus*, 97.

Samaritan village refused hospitality to Jesus, and the disciples sought permission from Jesus to call down fire from heaven to destroy the inhabitants. Although Jesus rebukes the disciples, the incident eloquently portrays the bitterness between the two groups.

It is against this backdrop of mutual hostility that the parable comes into focus. While the parable does not explicitly identify the victim, the fact that he was in Judean territory, between Jerusalem and Jericho, suggests that he is a Jew. Very little information, in fact, is given about the man, other than the violent details of his assault, which includes physical beating and the humiliation of being stripped of his clothing. Two other figures also make brief appearances in the story: a priest and Levite. Here the Jewish identity of these figures is clearer; both were representatives of the Jewish Temple personnel tasked with performing the varied sacrificial activities that took place in the Jerusalem Temple. Both of these men, upon seeing the injured fellow countryman, do what many people would be tempted to do in a similar situation: they "passed by on the other side" (Luke 10:31–32). The parable does not explain their motivations for neglecting the injured man. Such silence makes it possible for different hearers of the parable to insert themselves imaginatively into the story. In effect, readers are invited to ask themselves what feelings this scene might create in them, and what they would do in the same situation.

No ambiguity surrounds the ethnic and religious identity of the next character in the parable, "a Samaritan" (Luke 10:33). While we do not know what motivated the priest and Levite to pass by the victim, we are given immediate insight into the emotional response of the Samaritan, who feels "pity" for the victim. This response is surprising. Travelling in an area far from his own home turf, the Samaritan might be already on edge, and the sight of a beaten and naked man would elicit even more anxiety on his part. More surprising still is that the Samaritan's pity translates into concrete acts of bodily compassion that transcend the moment and cascade into commitments of extended long-term care for the well-being of the victim: "Then he put him on his animal, brought him to an inn, and took care of him. The next day he took out two denarii, gave them to the innkeeper, and said, 'Take care of him; and when I come back, I will repay you whatever more you spend'" (10:34–35). What makes the Samaritan a model of neighborly love is the fact that his love is consistent and ongoing. Something more than a one-time act of compassion is at play here that speaks to the possibility of a relationship that has the potential to grow into an unexpected future. This is the deeper significance of Jesus' invitation to the lawyer, "Go and do likewise" (10:37).

Just as important to notice, however, is that the Samaritan not only makes provision for the injured man's health; he also promises to return. Here lies what is perhaps the most intriguing element of this challenging story. There emerges a hint, however small, that the future may hold the promise of an ongoing relationship between these two men that will transcend the historic animosity between them. And this is perhaps the most important lesson in common life for Luke's community to consider. Can they be a community where love is shown not simply to like-minded persons but to those considered hated enemies? And can that love have the quality of consistent presence? Nothing less is possible if the community is to live out a truly counter-cultural common life together.

Summary

This chapter has examined the theme of common life in Luke's Gospel as it appears in both the Lukan infancy and journey narratives. Working with the conceptual category of legitimation, the chapter explored how Luke uses the characters within the infancy narrative to both describe and affirm the nature of his community's common life together. Then the role of common life in the journey narrative was discussed by interpreting two parables, unique to Luke's Gospel, where the theme of reconciliation appears. In both the journey narrative as well as the infancy narrative the counter-cultural character of the community's common life is both celebrated and offered as a challenge to strive toward.

Questions for Review

1. Why might the social makeup of Luke-Acts' audience help explain the motivation behind this distinctive two-volume work?

2. What role does the concept of salvation play in Luke's infancy narrative?

3. What are some of the specific teaching lessons found in the Lukan journey narrative?

Questions for Reflection

1. Reflecting on the characters found in Luke's infancy narrative, what might be similarly marginalized groups today? What would salvation as reversal look like for them?

2. In what specific ways might the parables of reconciliation addressed in this chapter be applied to issues of common life in the modern world?

3. Can you think of any other stories in Luke's journey narrative that might touch on the topic of common life?

For Further Reading

Borg, Marcus J., and John Dominic Crossan. *The First Paul: Reclaiming the Radical Visionary behind the Church's Conservative Icon.* New York: HarperOne, 2009.

Bovon, François. *Luke 1: A Commentary on the Gospel of Luke 1:1–9:50.* Translated by Christine M. Thomas. Hermeneia. Minneapolis: Fortress, 2002.

Brown, Raymond E. *Responses to 101 Questions on the Bible.* New York: Paulist Press, 1990.

Carroll, John T. *Luke: A Commentary.* Louisville: Westminster John Knox, 2012.

Esler, Philip Frances. *Community and Gospel in Luke-Acts: The Social and Political Implications of Lucan Theology.* Cambridge, UK: Cambridge University Press, 1987.

Green, Joel B. *The Theology of the Gospel of Luke.* Cambridge, UK: Cambridge University Press, 1995.

Gutiérrez, Gustavo. *We Drink from Our Own Wells: The Spiritual Journey of a People.* Translated by Matthew J. O'Connell. Maryknoll, NY: Orbis, 2003.

Hartin, Patrick J. *Exploring the Spirituality of the Gospels.* Collegeville, MN: Liturgical Press, 2010.

Hooker, Morna D. *Beginnings: Keys That Open the Gospels.* Harrisburg, PA: Trinity, 1997.

Johnson, Luke Timothy. *The Gospel of Luke.* Edited by Daniel J. Harrington, SJ. Sacra Pagina 3. Collegeville, MN: Liturgical Press, 1991.

Levine, Amy-Jill. *Short Stories by Jesus: The Enigmatic Parables of a Controversial Rabbi.* New York: HarperOne, 2014.

Miller, Amanda. "Bridge Work and Seating Charts: A Study of Luke's Ethics of Wealth, Poverty, and Reversal." *Interpretation* 68, no. 4 (2014): 416–27.

Pelikan, Jaroslav. *Jesus through the Centuries: His Place in the History of Culture.* New York: Harper, 1985.

Perkins, Pheme. *Introduction to the Synoptic Gospels.* Grand Rapids: Eerdmans, 2007.

Pervo, Richard. *Dating Acts: Between the Evangelists and the Apologists.* Santa Rosa, CA: Polebridge, 2006.

Shüssler Fiorenza, Elizabeth. *Bread Not Stone: The Challenge of Feminist Biblical Interpretation.* Boston: Beacon, 1984.

Thompson, Richard P. "Luke-Acts: The Gospel of Luke and the Acts of the Apostles." In *Blackwell Companion to the New Testament*, edited by David E. Aune, 319–43. Chichester, UK; London; Malden, MA: Wiley Blackwell, 2010.

Tobin, Thomas H. *The Spirituality of Paul.* Eugene, OR: Wipf & Stock, 1987.

Van Unnik, W. C. "Luke-Acts: A Storm Center in Contemporary Scholarship." In *Studies in Luke-Acts*, edited by Leander E. Keck and J. Louis Martyn, 15–32. Nashville: Abingdon, 1966.

Walters, Patricia. *The Assumed Authorial Unity of Luke and Acts: A Reassessment of the Evidence.* Cambridge, UK: Cambridge University Press, 2009.

Encountering John

The Mission of the Word of God in the Lives of the Children of God

The final New Testament Gospel to be explored in this study is the Gospel according to John, also known as the Fourth Gospel. As popular today as it was in antiquity, this Gospel preserves some of the best-known stories about Jesus. Only in this Gospel does Jesus wash the feet of his disciples (John 13:3–11), change water into wine (2:1–11), raise a corpse that had lain buried for four days in a tomb (11:1–44), converse with a Samaritan woman (4:7–42), and carry his own cross (19:17). Celebrated by many Christians for its exalted portrait of the Son of God, the Fourth Gospel is treasured just as widely for its intensely human vignettes of Jesus. In John's Gospel Jesus weeps (11:35), loves, (11:3, 36; 13:23; 19:26; 21:7, 20), calls his disciples friends (15:14), and even seeks assurance from a disciple that he is loved (21:15). Perhaps only in

The Metropolitan Museum of Art, Gift of J. Pierpont Morgan, 1917

Imagery from Ezekiel's vision of four "living creatures" before God's throne (Ezek. 1:5-11) was taken up in Christian iconography to represent the Four Gospels, as in this eleventh-century ivory plaque. The creature resembling an eagle is associated with John's Gospel, and also represents Jesus' divine status.

Mark's Gospel do we encounter a portrait of Jesus in any way comparable to the human realism that we see in John.

Few other Christian writings have played a more prominent role in the shaping of normative Christian beliefs and contemporary receptions of Jesus. The fourth-century framers of classical Christian doctrines such as the Trinity gave pride of place to John, pointing to those passages that they took as offering scriptural support for the argument that the Father and Son were of one and the same nature. More recently, both the rich symbolism and narrative artistry of the Fourth Gospel have attracted the attention of numerous biblical scholars, as have the many episodes in the Gospel that portray strong female characters who model authentic discipleship.[1]

The Beloved Disciple

As is the case with the Synoptic Gospels (Matthew, Mark, and Luke), the Gospel of John originally circulated as an anonymous text. By the latter half of the second century, however, a tradition emerged that linked the Fourth Gospel to the figure of the disciple John, one of the sons of Zebedee and one of the original Twelve. Also attested by the second century is the identification of the disciple John with the nameless Beloved Disciple who appears several times in the narrative beginning in chapter 13 (13:23-25; 19:26; 20:2; 21:7, 20). While these traditional claims are impossible to disprove, it is significant that a majority of the references to this mysterious disciple are intentionally open-ended and occur at pivotal junctures in the story. This suggests that the Beloved Disciple is meant to function as a highly symbolic figure who, from the perspective of the author, embodies the ideal response to the significance of the events of Jesus' life and death and resurrection.

---

1. See Craig R. Koester, *Symbolism in the Fourth Gospel: Meaning, Mystery, Community*, 2nd ed. (Minneapolis: Fortress, 2003), 1–32; Alan Culpepper, *Anatomy of the Fourth Gospel: A Study in Literary Design* (Philadelphia: Fortress, 1983), 15–49; Elizabeth A. Johnson, *Truly Our Sister: A Theology of Mary in the Communion of Saints* (New York: Continuum, 2006), 291–93.

The Gospel of John affords one the opportunity to pursue a broad range of topics for study. Given, however, the focus of this study on the topics of religious experience and common life, it is necessary to be selective. In this chapter, significant attention will be given to the role that the Prologue to John's Gospel (1:1–18) plays for understanding the theme of religious experience. In much the same way that the infancy narratives function in the Gospels of Matthew and Luke to provide privileged information to the reader regarding the deeper significance of Jesus' identity, the Prologue to John's Gospel gives expression to the religious experience that brought the Johannine community into existence, namely, the perception of the presence of God as revealed in the words and deeds of Jesus. The remainder of the chapter then examines representative episodes from the two major sections of the Fourth Gospel that are especially illustrative of the themes of religious experience and common life. These are the scene of Jesus' encounter with Nicodemus (3:1–21), the story of the encounter of Jesus with the Samaritan woman (4:1–42), and the account of the final discourse of Jesus with the disciples (13:1–17:26). Throughout this analysis an effort will be made to refer to other relevant material from the narrative of the Fourth Gospel that further illumines these themes.

Miraculous "Signs"

One of the more striking features of the Fourth Gospel relates to how the author shapes the traditions associated with Jesus as a miracle worker. Compared to the Synoptic Gospels, the Fourth Gospel has Jesus performing fewer miracles and these are consistently and positively described as "signs." There are a total of seven miraculous signs found in the first major division of John's Gospel (John 1:19-12:50). While several of these miracle accounts have parallels to similar miracles recorded in the Synoptic Gospels (4 and 5 below), others are unique to the Fourth Gospel (1 and 7 below). Such instances of similarity and difference raise interesting questions about the degree to which the author of the Fourth Gospel was familiar with the contents of Matthew,

Continued

Miraculous "Signs" *Continued*

Mark, and Luke. Scholars remain divided in their assessment of this issue.

The role that the signs of Jesus play in the Fourth Gospel is complex. On the one hand, the purpose of the signs is to promote belief in Jesus (see John 2:11; 4:43-54; 6:14; 20:30-31). On the other hand, passages in the Fourth Gospel seem to regard any response of faith that is based solely on the evidence of signs as inadequate (2:23-24; 4:48). Indeed, several passages suggest that it is attentiveness to the words or speech of Jesus that constitutes what for the author is the ideal response of faith (see 4:42, 50).

The Seven Miraculous Signs of the Gospel of John

1. The Changing of Water into Wine at the Wedding at Cana (2:1-11)

2. The Healing of the Official's Son (4:46-54)

3. The Healing of the Crippled Man (5:1-9)

4. The Feeding of the Five Thousand (6:1-14)

5. The Walking on the Sea (6:16-21)

6. The Healing of the Man Blind from Birth (9:1-12)

7. The Raising of Lazarus (11:1-44)

The Structure of the Fourth Gospel: The Book of Signs and the Book of Glory

Before examining the link that the Fourth Gospel makes between religious experience and common life, it might prove helpful to make some preliminary observations about the literary structure of John. The Fourth Gospel can be divided into at least two principal divisions. The focus of the first half of the Gospel is on the words and deeds of Jesus that reveal the close relationship that exists between the Son and the Father while the second half of the Gospel dwells extensively on the significance of the events associated with the suffering and death of Jesus.[2]

Following immediately upon the Prologue (John 1:1–18), John's account of the public career of Jesus spans the first twelve chapters of the narrative (1:19–12:50). Lending structural coherence to these chapters is a recurring geographical theme that portrays Jesus making several journeys from Galilee to Jerusalem for the purpose of celebrating both named and unnamed Jewish religious festivals. As he journeys back and forth through the regions of Galilee and Judea, Jesus performs a total of seven miracles that the narrator designates as signs. Four of these miracles are healing stories (4:46–54; 5:1–9; 9:1–12; 11:1–44) in which Jesus restores persons to physical wholeness, while three of the miracles function essentially as examples of nature miracles (2:1–11; 6:1–14; 6:16–21). Only two of these miracle accounts, the feeding of the five thousand (6:1–14) and Jesus walking on the sea (6:16–21), have significant parallels in the Synoptic Gospels. The first of Jesus' signs takes place in the village of Cana during a wedding celebration where Jesus turns water into wine (2:1–11) while the raising of Lazarus from the dead constitutes the seventh and final miracle story (11:1–44).

Woven into the account of the miracles of Jesus are several long speeches where Jesus elaborates on the deeper, spiritual meaning of his signs.[3] For example, in the discourse that follows the story of the feeding of the five thousand (John 6:22–65), Jesus tries to lead the crowds to the deeper understanding that the bread he had multiplied for them refers to himself, in particular his sacrificial death that will result in eternal life for anyone who believes in him (6:47–51). Many find these speeches in the Fourth Gospel both in regard to their tone and content quite dissimilar from the way Jesus speaks in the Synoptic Gospels. In place of teachings that focus on the kingdom of God or the dangers of wealth, there appear instead overtly self-referential statements in which Jesus applies to himself highly symbolic claims:

2. In a sense, then, one can reasonably speak of four divisions: the Prologue (1:1–18), the Book of Signs (1:19–12:50), the Book of Glory (13:1–20:31), and the Epilogue (21:1–25). For these divisions, see Francis J. Moloney, *The Gospel of John*, ed. Daniel J. Harrington, SJ, Sacra Pagina 4 (Collegeville, MN: Liturgical Press), 23.

3. The longest are the Bread of Life Discourse (John 6:22–59) and the long speech given at the Festival of Booths (7:1–8:59).

"I am the bread of life" (6:35), "I am the light of the world" (8:12; 9:5), "I am the gate for the sheep" (10:7, 9), "I am the resurrection and the life" (11:25), "I am the way, and the truth, and the life" (14:6), to name just a few such claims. Observing that this part of the narrative focuses largely on the miracles of Jesus conceived as signs, Raymond Brown famously designated this first major division of John's Gospel as the "Book of Signs."[4] Through a narrative account of the deeds and words of Jesus, the first half of the narrative dramatizes the fundamental religious proclamation of the Fourth Gospel, which is that Jesus reveals the glory or presence of God.

This proclamation is first enacted in the narrative through the story of the changing of water into wine at the wedding of Cana, the first of the signs that Jesus performs in the Fourth Gospel:

> On the third day there was a wedding in Cana of Galilee, and the mother of Jesus was there. Jesus and his disciples had also been invited to the wedding. When the wine gave out, the mother of Jesus said to him, "They have no wine." And Jesus said to her, "Woman, what concern is that to you and to me? My hour has not yet come." His mother said to the servants, "Do whatever he tells you." Now standing there were six stone water-jars for the Jewish rites of purification, each holding twenty or thirty gallons. Jesus said to them, "Fill the jars with water." And they filled them up to the brim. He said to them, "Now draw some out, and take it to the chief steward." So they took it. When the steward tasted the water that had become wine, and did not know where it came from (though the servants who had drawn the water knew), the steward called the bridegroom and said to him, "Everyone serves the good wine first, and then the inferior wine after the guests have become drunk. But you have kept the good wine until now." Jesus did this, the first of his signs, in Cana of Galilee, and revealed his glory; and his disciples believed in him. (John 2:1–11)

Although this particular miracle account has no exact parallel in any of the other Gospels, both the setting of the story at a banquet

---

4. Raymond E. Brown, *The Gospel According to John I-XII*, Anchor Bible Commentary 29 (New York: Doubleday, 1966), cxxxix. See also, Moloney, *The Gospel of John*, 23.

as well as the reference to the bridegroom recall traditional themes found elsewhere in the Gospel tradition (Mark 2:18–22). The scene is also notable for its inclusion of the mother of Jesus, who is always unnamed in the Fourth Gospel (see John 19:26–27). She appears in this story as a woman of agency and initiative, addressing the potentially embarrassing oversight of an insufficient supply of wine for the wedding feast (John 2:3).[5] In the process she also models the ideal response of discipleship by trusting the word of Jesus (John 2:5).

Placed first in the list of the seven signs performed by Jesus, the Cana episode is programmatic for the narrative as a whole, intimating major themes that will be treated later in the Gospel. Prominent in this regard is the foreshadowing of the death of Jesus. The only other place in the Fourth Gospel where the mother of Jesus is mentioned is at the foot of the cross as Jesus is dying (John 19:26–27). Also functioning to foreshadow the events of the suffering and death of Jesus is the first reference in the Gospel to the theme of the hour: "When the wine gave out, the mother of Jesus said to him, 'They have no wine.' And Jesus said to her, 'Woman, what concern is that to you and to me? My hour has not yet come'" (2:3–4; see also 7:30). As will be discussed later in this chapter, once the reader arrives at chapter 13 it is made clear that the "hour" represents the death of Jesus (13:1). Finally, whatever may be the precise theological point of mentioning the six jars containing water for the Jewish rites of purification (2:6), the reference to Jewish ritual activity itself underscores the intense interest the Fourth Gospel displays in having Jesus replicate the religious symbols and practices of the Jewish faith.

The story quickly draws the attention of the reader to the event of the transformation of the water into wine. Significantly, the transformation itself is not described; what is described is the overflowing abundance of the wine (John 2:7) as well as its exceptional quality (2:10). In the Jewish Scriptures, wine—as well as feasting in general—could be employed as a symbol for the new age when God would transform the creation.[6] Such symbolism is undoubtedly present in the story. At the same time, the slightly humorous reference to drunkenness in verse 10 reveals perhaps an even more

---

5. See Andrew T. Lincoln, *The Gospel According to John*, Black's New Testament Commentary 4 (London and New York: Continuum, 2005), 127.

6. See Lincoln, *The Gospel According to John*, 129.

important element to the overall meaning of the scene. The occasion of the story is a wedding celebration, with all the joy and promise such an occasion evokes. Then as today the consumption of wine can contribute significantly to the enhancing of the feelings of joy and fullness of life often attendant upon such a celebration. With this association in mind, the miracle sign of the changing of water into wine at the wedding of Cana functions to reveal Jesus as a figure who in his very person is the source of abundant life, the life that the Fourth Gospel will go on to describe as the refreshing gift of eternal life (4:14; 7:37–38). Adding a deeper and more enigmatic irony to this symbolism, however, are the suggestive hints to the imminent events of the suffering and death of Jesus. The deeper one journeys into the narrative, the more it becomes clear that the abundant life Jesus offers is offered precisely through his death (see 19:34).

The Book of Signs also prominently displays an array of memorable characters who interact with Jesus in highly personal ways. Several of these characters share certain features that make them representative types. For example, the stories of the paralyzed man (John 5:2–18), the royal official's son (4:46–54), and the blind man (9:1–41) introduce characters who are physically afflicted in some manner and who each receive from Jesus the gift of physical wholeness. At the same time, the three characters respond to Jesus in ways that show very different levels of understanding and acceptance of Jesus. The royal official and the blind man show remarkable levels of faith and insight, respectively. The royal official needs only the word of Jesus to trust that his son will be healed (4:48–50), while the man whose sight is restored ultimately identifies Jesus as Lord and worships him (9:38). By contrast, the healed paralytic informs on Jesus once he learns his name (5:13–15). Then there are other characters, such as the Pharisee Nicodemus (3:1–21) and the Samaritan woman at the well (4:1–42). Neither of them are depicted as suffering any physical affliction at all; they simply appear on the stage of the narrative and engage in highly personal, one-on-one conversations with Jesus, one of which leads nowhere while the other leads to remarkable insight.[7]

---

7. Stephen C. Barton, *The Spirituality of the Gospels* (Peabody, MA: Hendrickson, 1992), 115. See also Patrick J. Hartin, *Exploring the Spirituality of the Gospels* (Collegeville, MN: Liturgical Press, 2011), 67.

The second major division of the Fourth Gospel (John 13:1–17:26) is often designated by scholars as the Book of Glory. It contains both a final discourse by Jesus and the account of his arrest, suffering, and execution. The discourse is characterized by a strong tone of ethical formation. Anticipating his imminent death, Jesus imparts to his disciples during their final Passover supper together a vision of common life defined by friendship and above all self-sacrificial love for others (13:12–15).

Inscribed in this farewell discourse is also the experiential imprint of communal persecution (John 16:33) shaped by the rupture of previous religious commitments and intra-communal debate.[8] As J. Louis Martyn argues, the community behind the text of the Fourth Gospel seems to have been comprised of faithful Jews who at some point in the past had experienced expulsion from their synagogue as a consequence of their public confession about Jesus (see 9:22; 12:42).[9] Throughout the Farewell Discourse Jesus functions as the spokesperson for those in the community who publicly profess their faith in Jesus and as a consequence find themselves engaged in often antagonistic debate with fellow Jews: "But they will do all these things to you on account of my name, because they do not know him who sent me. . . . I have said these things to you to keep you from stumbling. They will put you out of the synagogues. Indeed, an hour is coming when those who kill you will think that by doing so they are offering worship to God. And they will do this because they have not known the Father or me" (15:21–16:3). This historical reconstruction explains a great deal of the tension and even ugliness in those scenes in the Fourth Gospel where Jesus is depicted as opposing members of his own ethnic and religious family. The crucial thing to note, however, is that these Jews should not be thought of as all Jews, everywhere, for all time, but as a relatively small group consisting mostly of powerful leaders in the first-century historical setting of John's Gospel.[10]

---

8. Harold W. Attridge, *Essays on John and Hebrews* (Grand Rapids: Baker, 2010), 6.

9. See the classic discussion in J. Louis Martyn, *History and Theology in the Fourth Gospel*, 3rd ed. (Louisville: Westminster John Knox, 2003).

10. Warren Carter, *John: Storyteller, Interpreter, Evangelist* (Peabody, MA: Hendrickson, 2006), 73. Tellingly, not all the references to the group called "the Jews" in John's Gospel are negative. See, for example, John 1:19; 5:1; 11:45; 12:9–11.

The Narrative Flow of John

First Division (1:1-12:50)
The Glory of God's Son Revealed

The Prologue (1:1-18) followed by account of the public ministry of Jesus defined by his miracle signs (1:19-12:50).

Second Division (13:1-17:26)
The Farewell Speech of God's Son

Conclusion of the public ministry of Jesus; Jesus withdraws to the circle of his disciples, providing them with final teachings, warnings, models of service, and the promise of the coming of the Spirit/Paraclete.

Third Division (18:1-21:25)
The Glorification of God's Son and the Advent of the Spirit

The account of the glorification of Jesus through his death (18:1-19:42); the Gospel concludes with an account of the empty tomb and resurrection appearance of Jesus to Mary Magdalene, followed by the bestowal of the Spirit to the disciples (20:1-31); a final resurrection appearance of Jesus to the disciples gathered at the Sea of Tiberias (21:1-25).

Religious Experience and the Prologue to John's Gospel: Jesus as the Disclosure of the Divine Presence

Each of the four Gospels is written in the conviction that the events of the life, death, and resurrection of Jesus of Nazareth embody the redeeming presence of the God of Israel in the world. While each of the evangelists interprets these events in his own unique manner, it is equally the case that the evangelists share in common the conviction that the man Jesus of Nazareth is a figure of divine significance. This is not to contend that the first Christians, who were Jewish after all, thought of Jesus as being in some way fully equal to God in terms of fundamental nature or essence. Such a view would have contradicted the committed monotheism that was a distinguishing mark of Jewish belief during the Second Temple period. Indeed, this belief emerges only centuries later in the development of Christian theological reflection. It does appear, however, that a perception of Jesus as deserving of the same worship as the God of Israel seems to have been a feature of primitive Christianity from the start.[11] That is, Jesus seems to have been accorded by the first Jewish Christians the same divine worship that first-century Jews normally reserved for the God of Israel alone. While such devotional practice is reflected in a number of places in the Synoptic Gospels, it is generally muted and seldom made explicit.[12] In Mark's Gospel, for example, the identity of Jesus is kept carefully hidden from the main characters in the narrative until the event of Jesus' death on the cross; only then is Jesus finally and fully revealed publicly as God's Son (Mark 15:39). By contrast, the Gospel of John explicitly identifies Jesus as a divine being who shares the same status and glory associated with the God of Israel (see John 1:1, 18; 5:18; 10:30, 33; 14:9). Such an explicit identification of Jesus with God is communicated to the reader right from the opening lines of the Gospel:

> In the beginning was the Word, and the Word was with God, and the Word was God. He was in the beginning with God. All things came into being through him, and without him not one thing came into being. What has come into being in him was life, and the life was the light of all people. The light shines in the darkness, and the darkness did not overcome it. (John 1:1–5)

These verses comprise the beginning of what is usually called the Prologue to John's Gospel and function to immerse the reader in an account of the origins of Jesus that is cosmic in its scope.[13] In contrast to the opening line of Mark's Gospel, where the language

---

11. See the important study on the subject by Larry W. Hurtado, *Lord Jesus Christ: Devotion to Jesus in Earliest Christianity* (Grand Rapids: Eerdmans, 2002).

12. For examples see Matt. 17:1–2; Mark 6:47–51; 9:2–3; Luke 9:28–29.

13. See Craig R. Koester, *The Word of Life: A Theology of John's Gospel* (Grand Rapids: Eerdmans, 2008), 8.

of the beginning (*archē*) refers simply to the commencement of the story itself (Mark 1:1), John's Prologue introduces the reader to the absolute beginning of time, what one might call the sphere of eternity. More dramatic still, the Prologue associates this absolute beginning with a mysterious figure identified simply as the Word or, in Greek, *Logos* (John 1:1).

Depending upon their conceptual background, different readers or listeners of the Prologue would have understood this term in different ways. The educated among John's audience may well have heard in this term echoes of Stoic philosophy, in which the concept of the Word or Logos referred to the divine principle understood to pervade the cosmos.[14] Others among the audience who were familiar with the Jewish Scriptures might have heard echoes of scriptural passages that celebrated the creative power of God's speech operative in the world.[15] One such passage might have been Isaiah 55:11: "So shall my word be that goes out from my mouth; it shall not return to me empty, but it shall accomplish that which I purpose, and succeed in the thing for which I sent it." And for those for whom the term bore no specific conceptual background there was always ready at hand the association taken from daily experience of the use of human speech to embody thought and thereby communicate with others.[16]

But what does any of this have to do with Jesus and, more specifically, to the question of his origin? To answer this question, it is important first of all to appreciate that the Fourth Gospel is in every way as intentionally crafted a narrative as are the other three canonical Gospels. In particular, one does well to recognize the presence in the Prologue of what one might call the voice of the narrator. As Alan Culpepper notes, one can think of the narrator as that invisible guide who helps the reader to perceive both the deeper significance of the events that are taking place in the narrative as well as the true motivations of characters within the narrative.[17] This device is commonly used in short stories, novels, and even contemporary films as a means to promote deeper understanding of issues such as

---

14. Lincoln, *The Gospel According to John*, 95.

15. Lincoln, *The Gospel According to John*, 94–95.

16. See Moloney, *The Gospel of John*, 95.

17. Culpepper, *Anatomy*, 16–20.

plot development.[18] By imparting to the reader the narrator's reliable understanding of the ultimate origins of Jesus, John's Prologue functions in much the same manner.[19]

The Prologue begins with the proclamation that the Word/Logos has existed from all eternity alongside God (John 1:1). The technical term that scholars use to convey this idea is *preexistence*. Although it is not until later in the Prologue that the narrator explicitly identifies the Word/Logos with the historical figure of Jesus of Nazareth (1:14), the original audience for whom the Fourth Gospel was written would have anticipated this connection, since it is likely that the identification of the Word with Jesus was already a central feature of their corporate worship life.[20] John's Prologue begins, then, by making the striking claim that in the sphere of eternity the Son of God has always existed in a completely spiritual, eternal manner. While the concept of preexistence likely appears in other New Testament texts (Phil. 2:6–7; Col. 1:15; Heb. 1:1–3; 5:7), it finds its most forceful expression here.

Surprising as it may seem in light of the monotheistic commitment of the first Christians, a precedent for thinking of Jesus in this way was already available in the form of Jewish scriptural interpretation that focused on the concept of the personified Wisdom of God. Important instances of this intellectual tradition appear both in the Jewish Scriptures (Prov. 8:22–31) as well as in Jewish texts closer to the time of the composition of the Fourth Gospel, such as the book of Wisdom and the book of Sirach. The following passage from the book of Wisdom provides a good example of the features that informed this tradition: "For Wisdom is more mobile than any motion; because of her pureness she pervades and penetrates all things. For she is a breath of the power of God. . . . She is a reflection of eternal light, a spotless mirror of the working of God. . . . She is more beautiful than the sun, and excels every constellation of the stars. Compared with the light she is found to be superior, for it is succeeded by the night,

---

18. Paul N. Anderson similarly notes, "The Prologue to the Gospel seeks to engage hearers and readers experientially in the story that follows." See Paul N. Anderson, *The Riddles of the Fourth Gospel: An Introduction to John* (Philadelphia: Fortress, 2011), 12.

19. Culpepper, *Anatomy*, 16–20.

20. A sizeable majority of scholars believe that much of the Prologue originated as a hymn that would have been sung in a liturgical setting of devotion to Jesus. See Brown, *The Gospel According to John I–XII*, 18–21.

By the first century CE, some Jewish literature depicted the "wisdom" of God as though it were a person, thereby paving the way for John's identification of Jesus as God's divine Logos ("word" or "reason"). Since the word for wisdom is grammatically feminine in both Greek (*sophia*) and Hebrew (*hokmah*), personified Wisdom was traditionally portrayed as female.

but against wisdom evil does not prevail" (Wis. 7:24–30). In this passage Wisdom is conceived as both expressive of God and intimately connected with all of creation. The same thought is expressed in John 1:4–5, where the light of Wisdom/the Logos, unlike natural light, is depicted as prevailing over darkness.

Wisdom is similarly presented in the book of Proverbs as existing with God from the very beginning and even taking a role in the creation of the cosmos (Prov. 8:22–31). On display in both these texts is the intellectual activity of the Jewish sages who strove to articulate the mystery of how the God of Israel, who is unlike anything in the creation, can at the same time be immanent within the creation. The concept of God's Wisdom personified was developed, therefore, as a way to bridge the distance between a God defined by transcendence, on the one hand, and the creation that was believed to have its source in this transcendence, on the other.

The early Christians creatively adapted the categories of Jewish Wisdom reflection to articulate the deeper significance of the origins of Jesus. Previous chapters discussed how the infancy narratives of Matthew and Luke reflect on the mystery of the origins of Jesus by employing the theological claim that the Son of God was conceived by the Spirit within the bounds of history. Building upon the conceptual category of personified Wisdom, the Prologue to John traces the origin of the Son even further back than that, beyond even the very beginning of time in the ineffable sphere of eternity. From this emphasis on the eternal status of the Word, there is only a small step to the implication that the Word is also divine, which is precisely the inference that the Prologue draws in the conclusion of verse 1 with the claim "and the Word was God" (John 1:1).

This verse exercised tremendous influence in later church debates concerning the relationship between God the Father and the Son. Consequently, it is crucial to be clear about what the Prologue is trying to say. The force of the claim is not that the Word shares an identical nature with God. This particular understanding emerges several centuries after John's Gospel was written, when the early church was debating the question, Should the Son be understood to be related to God as the most highly exalted creature among all creation, or is the relationship between the Father and Son something more like a union of substance?[21]

The Prologue, however, is not speaking of divine substance, but is trying to express the relation of the Word to God along the lines of the metaphor of human speech. Whenever one engages in a conversation with another person, one essentially reveals to the conversation partner the thoughts and feelings of one's inner self. Without recourse to speech, one's inner life remains unarticulated and largely hidden from others. By analogy, to state that the "Word was God" is to affirm that the Word articulates or reveals the essential character of the divine itself. The Word is understood to quite literally draw God forth into the open.[22] At root, then, the claim in view in the Prologue is decidedly functional in character. That is, the Word reveals everything that God is and in such a comprehensive fashion that the Word shares fundamentally the same status as God. This way of thinking about how Jesus can be identified with God also helps to shed light on the many passages one finds in later chapters

---

21. See Henry Chadwick, *The Early Church*, rev. ed. (New York: Penguin, 1993), 124.

22. The final verse of the Prologue in the NRSV reads, "No one has ever seen God. It is God the only Son, who is close to the Father's heart, who has made him known" (John 1:18). A more literal translation of the Greek verb translated as "made him known" might be "to lead forward or draw forth."

of the Fourth Gospel where Jesus repeatedly bases his claim of unity with God by insisting that the Son only speaks and acts in obedience to the will of God.[23] The narrator can attest that Jesus is divine, even God, because in accordance with the theological vision of the Fourth Gospel the essential shape and character of God are disclosed in the words and deeds of Jesus.

On display in the Prologue, then, is a clear testimony to the religious experience of the community for whom John's Gospel was written. While remaining true to their monotheistic commitment to a belief in the oneness of God, they have nonetheless experienced what can best be expressed as the disclosure of God all over again. The full measure of this experience is articulated—to the extent that it can be articulated at all—by verse 14 of the Prologue: "And the Word became flesh and lived among us, and we have seen his glory, the glory as of a Father's only son, full of grace and truth."

It may not be going too far to say that this verse functions as the theological thesis statement of the Fourth Gospel. It also, for all its conciseness, reveals a great deal about the theological commitment that both underlies and animates the distinctive common life of the Johannine community. As Elizabeth Johnson observes, the term "glory" signified in its Jewish context the notion of the radiance and splendor of God as revealed in visible manifestation.[24] Glory, therefore, is another way of speaking of the invisible presence of God made palpable in the world. Guided by this definition of glory, we might say that the narrator and the audience of the Fourth Gospel share the faith conviction that the eternal, invisible self-expression of God became embodied at a particular point in history in a particular Jewish man, Jesus of Nazareth.

It is important to be clear about the precise nature of this conviction. The claim being made in the Prologue is not that Jesus was in some objective sense a superhuman being whose glory would be self-evident to all who encountered him. The Gospel of John is quite clear that Jesus was in every respect an ordinary human being, one might even say exceedingly ordinary (see John 1:45–46;

---

23. See 5:19, 30, 36; 8:28–29; 14:10–11.

24. Elizabeth A. Johnson, *She Who Is: The Mystery of God in Feminist Theological Discourse* (New York: Crossroads, 1991), 85.

6:42; 7:5). Nevertheless, the community attests to have experienced in the words, deeds, death, and resurrection of this person the self-disclosure of God: "No one has ever seen God. It is God the only Son, who is close to the Father's heart, who has made him known" (1:18).

In a passage composed much earlier than the Fourth Gospel, the Apostle Paul captures remarkably well what the Prologue to John is attempting to convey when he describes the "knowledge of the glory of God" as manifested in the "face of Jesus Christ" (2 Cor. 4:6). For the narrator of the Prologue, as well as for the Apostle Paul, the experience of the self-disclosure of God is pictured as profoundly relational in character. That is, it is something like the experience one has when one looks upon the face of a friend or a beloved and recognizes another. Put another way, underlying the highly theological language of the Prologue is a deeply personal religious experience that is so affective and transformative that it calls into existence a new community: "He came to what was his own, and his own people did not accept him. But to all who received him, who believed in his name, he gave power to become children of God, who were born, not of blood or of the will of the flesh or of the will of man, but of God" (John 1:11–13). In this passage the theme of common life is given evocative expression through the corporate and highly personal metaphor, "children of God." With the aid of this strongly Jewish covenantal metaphor, the narrator celebrates how the faith perception of God's glory in Jesus has inaugurated a new community empowered and identified not through biological ties of kinship but through the power of God. As the narrative will go on to demonstrate, the circle of this family is indeed a wide one: all are included on the basis of a common experience of faith, whether they be Jews, Samaritans, or Gentiles, these being the primary ethnic and religious identity markers operative at the time when John's Gospel was written.

Common Life in the Book of Signs: The Encounter with Nicodemus

The Fourth Gospel displays an abiding concern to reflect on the topic of common life in a number of ways. Only in this Gospel, for example, do we encounter the evocative communal metaphors of Jesus as the Good Shepherd (John 10:11–18) and the true vine (15:1–11). On one level, both images reinforce for the community behind the text the idea that Jesus is the foundational source that has brought this new community into existence. But on a deeper level, the images also speak to the close personal sense of union with Jesus that the community presently experiences in light of what they perceive as the abiding presence of the resurrected Jesus in their lives. This is especially true with regard to the metaphor of the vine, an image that emphasizes not only that Jesus is the source of common life but that living in a new way is possible only if the community continues to participate in Jesus (15:4–11).[25] The same concern to link personal union with Jesus to the theme of common life is seen earlier in the narrative with the story of the call of the first disciples (1:35–51). There it appears that only after spending time with Jesus, literally remaining with him in personal relationship (1:39), are the disciples empowered to comprehend the deeper significance of who Jesus is.[26] This relationship of personal encounter is what enables the disciples to understand the deeper significance of the changing of water into wine at Cana. Unlike the crowds in chapter 6 who interpret the feeding in the wilderness simply as a sign about physical food and physical hunger, the disciples see beyond the joyous gift of wine to satisfy thirst and promote joy to a manifestation of the glory of the life of God (2:11).

The story of Jesus' encounter with Nicodemus offers an enlightening example of how the narrator of the Fourth Gospel weaves the theme of common life into the account of the signs that Jesus performs. Impressed with the signs that Jesus has performed while in Jerusalem for Passover, Nicodemus, a learned Pharisee and Jewish leader (John 3:1), seeks Jesus out to honor him as a rabbi, or teacher, who has come from God (3:2). On the face of it, this honorific title sounds positive; however, the brief conversation that follows between Nicodemus and Jesus adds a level of ambiguity to this promising first impression. The exchange itself is characterized by highly allusive language and no small measure of irony:

---

25. See the helpful discussion in Koester, *The Word of Life*, 195–96.

26. See Gustavo Gutiérrez, *We Drink from Our Own Wells: The Spiritual Journey of a People*, trans. Matthew J. O'Connell (Maryknoll, NY: Orbis, 1984), 38–42.

> Jesus answered him, "Very truly, I tell you, no one can see the kingdom of God without being born from above." Nicodemus said to him, "How can anyone be born after having grown old? Can one enter a second time into the mother's womb and be born?" Jesus answered, "Very truly, I tell you, no one can enter the kingdom of God without being born of water and Spirit. What is born of the flesh is flesh, and what is born of the Spirit is spirit." (John 3:3–6)

Throughout the encounter Nicodemus comes off as hopelessly obtuse, unable to decipher the deeper meaning of the assertions of Jesus concerning rebirth from above. The irony of the entire exchange is only heightened when Jesus—who later in the narrative will be described as uneducated (John 7:15)—directs an accusatory jibe at Nicodemus: "Are you a teacher of Israel, and yet you do not understand these things?" (3:10). The "things" are encompassed by the three topics of the kingdom of God, the activity of the Spirit, and the reality of religious rebirth. The repetition of the word "born" in Jesus' reply to Nicodemus recalls the earlier statement made in the Prologue that those who believed in Jesus received power to become children of God, "who were born, not of blood or of the will of the flesh or of the will of man, but of God" (1:12–13). As already noted, this passage from the Prologue likely reflects the conviction of the Johannine community that they now possess a new common life characterized by spiritual rebirth through the power of God. The new emphasis on the topic of birth from above found in the story of the encounter between Nicodemus and Jesus similarly has the idea of common life in view. Only now it is said that common life has something to do with the reality of the kingdom of God.

The concept of the kingdom of God was previously encountered in the discussion of the themes of religious experience and common life as these appear in Mark's Gospel. There it was noted that kingdom language in Mark is ambiguous in the sense that there are passages in Mark that envision the kingdom both as a future as well as a present reality. On one level, this same ambiguity is found also in the Fourth Gospel. Jesus' summary of his mission seems to point to a future reality: "For I have come down from heaven, not to do my own will, but the will of him who sent me. And this is the will of him who sent me, that I should lose nothing of all that he has given me, but raise it up on the last day. This is indeed the will of my Father, that all who see the Son and believe in him may have eternal life; and I will raise them up on the last day" (John 6:38–40). But, at the same time, John's Gospel gives far greater emphasis to the present aspect of the kingdom. Inheriting a traditional definition of the kingdom as an essentially transcendent reality that will transform the world in the age to come, the Fourth Gospel typically collapses the futurity of the gift of the kingdom into a gift that can essentially be attained right now.

The gift of the kingdom is linked precisely with a particular form of religious experience, namely, the experience of receiving eternal life through the response of faith in Jesus (John 3:15, 36; 6:40, 68; 11:25–26). In other words, in using the language of entering into the kingdom (3:3, 5), Jesus gives expression to how the community behind the Fourth Gospel understands themselves to be a community that has been empowered by God to live in a new way. This experience of divine empowerment ultimately has to do with another experience, namely, that of the activity of the Spirit: "Do not be astonished that I said to you, 'You must be born from above.' The wind blows where it chooses, and you hear the sound of it, but you do not know where it comes from or where it goes. So it is with everyone who is born of the Spirit" (3:7–8). Still overwhelmed by confusion, Nicodemus can only respond, "How can these things be?" (3:9).

As already noted, the language of the Spirit is linked in the Jewish tradition with the presence of God. Throughout the Fourth Gospel the Spirit is uniquely connected with the power of Jesus' presence unleashed through the events of his death and subsequent resurrection to new life (John 7:39; 14:25–26; 16:7, 13; 20:22). Likewise the link between the ideas of rebirth, the Spirit, and the kingdom of God becomes apparent in this story toward the end of Jesus' speech: "And just as Moses lifted up the serpent in the wilderness, so must the Son of Man be lifted up, that whoever believes in him may have eternal life. For God so loved the world that he gave his only Son, so that everyone who believes in him may not perish but may have eternal life" (3:14–16). Ultimately, it is the death of Jesus, conceived as his glorification, that paradoxically opens the way into the kingdom of God at the center of this new common life (10:16–17; 11:51; 17:20–21). Everything about the encounter between Nicodemus and Jesus functions to confirm for the reader that the title of teacher given by Nicodemus to Jesus is an inadequate honorific to describe the nature of the gift offered by the Son (see 4:10). While nothing in this story suggests that Nicodemus opposes Jesus or the claims he makes for himself, neither is there any indication that Nicodemus commits himself to Jesus. Although Nicodemus appears again near the end of Jesus' life (7:50–51) and for a final time after Jesus dies (19:39), the reader is never told that Nicodemus remained with him. The story of the encounter between Jesus and the Samaritan woman, which immediately follows this story, describes a very different response to the gift Jesus offers.

Common Life in the Book of Signs: The Encounter with the Samaritan Woman

Warren Carter observes, "Consistently the male disciples are outperformed by a small number of women who often present examples of positive responses—believing in or entrusting themselves to Jesus."[27] This observation is admirably illustrated in the story of the encounter of Jesus with the Samaritan woman at the well (John 4:7–42). Interacting somewhat playfully with a scene familiar from the biblical narrative where a Jewish patriarch encounters his soon-to-be spouse (see Gen. 24:42–67; 29:1–28), the narrator tells a story in which an ever-deepening relationship in faith develops between Jesus and this anonymous woman. Although the story does not culminate in marriage between Jesus and the woman, a bond of common life does emerge that is based on belief in Jesus (John 4:39–42). It is a story that in many ways is meant to function as the mirror opposite of the exchange between Jesus and Nicodemus, even to the symbolic juxtaposition of the temporal markers of night and day.[28] While Nicodemus never progresses beyond a rudimentary insight based on signs,

---

27. Carter, *John*, 78.

28. See Moloney, *The Gospel of John*, 91.

Jesus speaks with the Samaritan woman at the well in this fourth-century fresco from the catacombs of Via Latina, Rome. In John's account, this anonymous woman comes to a more profound understanding of Jesus than does Nicodemus, "a teacher of Israel," in the previous chapter.

the Samaritan woman more than progresses in her understanding of Jesus' identity without any accompanying signs; indeed her faithful acceptance of Jesus, like that of the royal official—and the blind man, for that matter—is engendered solely on the basis of the words of Jesus (4:27–29). Likewise, it is initially on the basis of her testimony in conversation with fellow Samaritans in her village (4:39) that others in her community seek Jesus out, remain with him (4:40), and ultimately proclaim Jesus as the Savior of the world (4:42). The identity of both the woman and her fellow villagers as alien Samaritans (4:9) adds another dimension of significance to the vision of common life articulated in the story. The power of the kingdom of God made available right now is capacious enough for the dwelling of everyone, including those who might be seen as occupying the religious and ethnic margins.

Common Life in the Book of Glory:
The Farewell Discourse of the Fourth Gospel
(13:1-17:26)

We have already established that the term "glory" is used in the Fourth Gospel to refer to the presence of God revealed in and through the signs and words of Jesus. While there are anticipations throughout the earlier chapters of the Gospel of the suffering and death that Jesus ultimately will face, these events are now brought explicitly into the open of the story world beginning in chapter 13: "Now before the festival of Passover, Jesus knew that his hour had come to depart from this world and go to the Father. Having loved his own who were in the world, he loved them to the end" (John 13:1).

Set within the context of a final Passover meal with his disciples, the farewell discourse serves several different purposes for the narrator. First, the speech establishes the correct perspective from which to evaluate the events of the suffering and death of Jesus. Like all the evangelists, the author of the Fourth Gospel had to reckon honestly with the apparently shameful and humiliating fate that Jesus suffered. On the face of it, the crucifixion of Jesus would seem to discredit the claim that Jesus does in fact reveal the glory or presence of God. The narrator of the Fourth Gospel addresses this apparent disqualification of Jesus by interpreting his death as the very conduit through which the presence of God is mediated in all its fullness: "I did not say these things to you from the beginning, because I was with you. But now I am going to him who sent me. . . . Nevertheless I tell you the truth: it is to your advantage that I go away, for if I do not go away, the Advocate will not come to you; but if I go, I will send him to you" (John 16:4–7).

In order to appreciate the meaning of the term "advocate," one must recall an earlier passage in the Gospel when, during the religious festival of Booths, Jesus invites the crowds to satisfy their spiritual thirst by believing in him (John 7:37–38). As if sensing the need for additional interpretation, the narrator clarifies for the reader in verse 39 that the water to which Jesus refers is in fact the Spirit of God, the Spirit that as yet had not come since Jesus had not yet been glorified. It becomes clear in the farewell discourse that the link that the narrator draws between the glorification of Jesus and the sending of the Spirit refers to a new way in which Jesus and God will now be present to the community. Far from disqualifying Jesus as the revelation of the Father (14:8–11), the death of Jesus serves as the glorious passageway to a new level of existence that Jesus now has as a result of being raised from the dead (20:19–22). Alive in a new way as a result of being raised to a new level of existence with God, Jesus, through the Spirit, will now accompany the community forever, all the while guiding their understanding and renewing their lives (15:5; 16:12–13).

In addition to reevaluating the death of Jesus as an event of ultimate glory and triumph (John 16:33), the farewell discourse also functions to articulate the principles that are to inform the common life of the community animated by the Spirit of Jesus. Foremost in this regard is love (13:34–35; 15:9–11). The love envisioned by Jesus, however, is of a particular character: it is characterized by the renouncing of any desire to rise above others or to seek the esteem of others. Jesus enacts this kind of love through the embodied example of the washing of the disciples' feet:

> Now before the festival of the Passover, Jesus knew that his hour had come to depart from this world and go to the Father. Having loved his own who were in the world, he loved them to the end. The devil had already put it into the heart of Judas son of Simon Iscariot to betray him. And during supper Jesus, knowing that the Father had given all things into his hands, and that he had come from God and was going to God, got up from the table, took off his outer robe, and tied a towel around himself. Then he poured water into a basin and began to wash the disciples' feet and to wipe them with the towel that was tied around him. He came to Simon Peter, who said to him, "Lord, are you going to wash my feet?" Jesus answered, "You do not know now what I am doing, but later you will understand." Peter said to him, "You will never wash my feet." Jesus answered, "Unless I wash you, you have no share with me." . . . After he had washed their feet, had put on his robe, and had returned to the table, he said to them, "Do you know what I have done to you? You call me Teacher and Lord—and you are right,

for that is what I am. So if I, your Lord and Teacher, have washed your feet, you also ought to wash one another's feet. For I have set you an example, that you also should do as I have done to you." (John 13:1–15)

To appreciate the subversive quality of this story in the social terms of the ancient world, one should recognize that Jesus is of higher status than the disciples. He is, in short, their teacher and Lord with all the authority and implied honorable status those titles would have evoked in John's first-century Mediterranean setting. And yet Jesus assumes in this story the posture of a slave, and even more radically, a semi-naked slave, who performs the useful but hardly glamorous task of washing the unpleasant detritus of ancient streets off the feet of his guests, the disciples. While the foot-washing scene plays a very clear role in foreshadowing the self-giving that Jesus will enact through his death, it also has profound implications for the nature of common life espoused by the narrator of the Fourth Gospel. The foot-washing story is not a celebration of self-denigration. Instead, the focus is on a new way of relating to others in common life. Whatever particular social grouping is in view, seeking after personal power and esteem is so prevalent that it seems almost taken for granted that every form of communal gathering will of necessity have winners and losers within its ranks. This was as true in the first-century world as it is today. The love envisioned in the foot-washing scene in the farewell discourse is akin to the quality of love described in the following passage from *Les Mis*:

One day, that man who considered himself "a philosopher," the senator mentioned before, said to the bishop, "See now, what the world shows us: each fighting against all others; the strongest man is the best man. Your love one another is stupidity." "Well," replied Monsieur Bienvenu without arguing, "if it is stupidity, the soul ought to shut itself up in it, like the pearl in the oyster."[29]

---

29. Victor Hugo, *Les Misérables*, trans. Lee Fahnestock and Norman MacAfee (New York: Signet, 2013), 57.

Summary

Central to the religious experience that is articulated in the Fourth Gospel is the conviction that the glory or presence of God is disclosed in the person of Jesus of Nazareth. First expressed in the Prologue, the theme of the disclosure of God in Jesus is shown to have communal significance through the stories of Jesus' encounters with various characters in the Book of Signs, in particular the figures of Nicodemus and the Samaritan woman at the well. In both these stories the experience of the Johannine community as being in personal union with Jesus is dramatized in mirror opposite ways. Challenged to rethink his notions of how one enters the kingdom through being empowered by the Spirit and receiving the gift of eternal life, Nicodemus balks and only goes so far in his encounter with Jesus. The conversation between them essentially stops. By contrast, the Samaritan woman continues to engage Jesus, despite her confusion, and ultimately progresses both in terms of her insight and personal encounter with him. Finally, both the themes of divine disclosure and common life as union with Jesus are refracted through the prism of the event of the death of Jesus, which is cast in the Fourth Gospel as the definitive expression of God's glory in the Son. This theological conviction is then given practical expression through the story of the foot-washing, which dramatizes the kind of conduct that is empowered by the life-giving Spirit of the resurrected Jesus.

Questions for Review

1. What are some of the most distinctive features of the nature of religious experience and common life as described in the Fourth Gospel?

2. In what ways does the Prologue to the Fourth Gospel influence the way in which the reader interprets the rest of John's Gospel?

3. What are the major features of the Book of Signs found in the Fourth Gospel?

4. Why is Jewish reflection on the role of Wisdom important for understanding the conceptual background of the Prologue to John's Gospel?

Questions for Reflection

1. Of the four Gospels, where would you rank the Fourth Gospel in terms of your level of interest? Why?

2. Does the story of the encounter between Jesus and the Samaritan woman aid contemporary efforts at ecumenical dialogue between different religious traditions? If so, how? If not, why not?

For Further Reading

Anderson, Paul N. *The Riddles of the Fourth Gospel: An Introduction to John*. Philadelphia: Fortress, 2011.

Ashton, John. *Understanding the Fourth Gospel*. London: Clarendon, 1991.

Attridge, Harold W. *Essays on John and Hebrews*. Grand Rapids: Baker, 2010.

Barton, Stephen C. *The Spirituality of the Gospels*. Peabody, MA: Hendrickson, 1992.

Brown, Raymond. *The Gospel According to John I-XII*. Anchor Bible Commentary 29. New York: Doubleday, 1966.

Carter, Warren. *John: Storyteller, Interpreter, Evangelist*. Peabody, MA: Hendrickson, 2006.

Chadwick, Henry. *The Early Church*. Rev. ed. New York: Penguin, 1993.

Culpepper, R. Alan. *Anatomy of the Fourth Gospel: A Study in Literary Design*. Philadelphia: Fortress, 1983.

Hartin, Patrick J. *Exploring the Spirituality of the Gospels*. Collegeville, MN: Liturgical Press, 2011.

Hurtado, Larry W. *Lord Jesus Christ: Devotion to Jesus in Earliest Christianity*. Grand Rapids: Eerdmans, 2002.

Johnson, Elizabeth A. *She Who Is: The Mystery of God in Feminist Theological Discourse*. New York: Crossroad, 1993.

———. *Truly Our Sister: A Theology of Mary in the Communion of Saints*. New York: Continuum, 2006.

Koester, Craig R. *Symbolism in the Fourth Gospel: Meaning, Mystery, Community*. 2nd ed. Minneapolis: Fortress, 2003.

———. *The Word of Life: A Theology of John's Gospel.* Grand Rapids: Eerdmans, 2008.

Lincoln, Andrew T. *The Gospel According to John.* Black's New Testament Commentary 4. London and New York: Continuum, 2005.

Martyn, J. Louis. *History and Theology in the Fourth Gospel.* 3rd ed. Louisville: Westminster John Knox, 2003.

Moloney, Francis J. *The Gospel of John.* Edited by Daniel J. Harrington, SJ. Sacra Pagina 4. Collegeville, MN: Liturgical Press, 1998.

6

Encountering Paul

Reflections on Reconstructing
the Historical Apostle

Approximately **twenty years after the crucifixion** of Jesus, the Apostle Paul recalled for a small cell of believers in the ancient city of Corinth the peculiar character of the proclamation that brought this community into existence: "When I came to you, brothers and sisters, I did not come proclaiming the mystery of God to you in lofty words or wisdom. For I decided to know nothing among you except Jesus Christ, and him crucified" (1 Cor. 2:1–2). How strange this figure must have seemed both to the streetwise and the sophisticated residents of the urban capital of the Roman province of Achaia? It was bad enough that the content of his message was foolish and offensive (1:23); his seeming reluctance or inability (2:3) to package his message in smooth

The Metropolitan Museum of Art, Gift of J. Pierpont Morgan, 1917

In this twelfth-century Byzantine medallion, Saint Paul holds a book in his left hand, hinting at the letters of Paul, which are now canonized in the New Testament.

rhetorical form only added to the palpable nonsense of his words. Yet something moved at least some in the city of Corinth to perceive a curious power and even wisdom in this spectacle (1:24–25). Quite inexplicably, some put their faith or trust (2:5) in the message of this man and in the man himself (4:15). A relationship formed and was thereafter nurtured through the medium of letters that served as encounters, sometimes strained and painful encounters, between a surrogate father and his children (4:14–15).

Several observations were made earlier in this study concerning the literary and thematic character of the letters of Paul. Comprising the earliest writings contained in the New Testament, these letters offer glimpses into some of the challenges and formative experiences faced by the first generation of Christians as they sought to live out their new identity within the multicultural and religiously pluralistic environment of the ancient Mediterranean world. Also to be found in these letters is something that is lacking in the Gospels, namely, first-person accounts from someone who was personally involved in many of the events and issues related in these texts. No writings of Jesus are known, of course, and the events attributed to him in the Gospels were recorded long after his own lifetime. Despite the fact that Paul's letters were edited and arranged into collections after his death, they still contain substantially the words and thoughts of the person who designated himself the Apostle to the Gentiles.[1]

The Paul of the Book of Acts and the Paul of the Letters

Relative to many other historical figures who are mentioned in the New Testament, an abundance of information about Paul is available. When assessing the value of this material for the purposes of historical reconstruction, however, it appears that not all of this data is equal.[2] In terms of the sheer amount of data that it preserves

---

1. The term "Gentiles" (Greek, *ethnē*) is used here as a collective term to designate the diverse populations of the ancient Mediterranean region that did not identify as either religiously or ethnically Jewish.

2. Since this study is meant to serve primarily as a focused supplement to introductory courses on the New Testament, many complex issues surrounding the historical Paul are treated in a summary manner only. For more detailed, yet accessible, discussions on these and other matters associated with the historical Paul, see Michael J. Gorman, *Apostle of the Crucified Lord: A Theological Introduction to Paul and His Letters*

about Paul, the Acts of the Apostles remains an important resource for reconstructing the Paul of history. The reader will recall that Acts functions as the second volume of a larger two-volume work that also includes the Gospel According to Luke. Although both texts have traditionally been regarded as having been written by the same author, the two works appear to represent two distinct literary genres. While Luke's Gospel displays features characteristic of the ancient genre of biography, Acts most closely epitomizes another literary genre recognizable in the ancient world, historiography.[3] As the New Testament's sole example of a general history, Acts provides a narrative account of the growth of the primitive Jesus movement from its commencement in the city of Jerusalem up until its emergence as a multi-ethnic religious movement spread throughout the Mediterranean world.

Although numerous characters appear in the book of Acts, Paul emerges from chapter 9 onward as the focal figure in the narrative. As a result of this attention lavished on Paul, a wealth of historical material concerning him can be gleaned from Acts. Some of this material, moreover, is found nowhere else. For example, Acts alone reports Paul's status as a Roman citizen (Acts 16:37; 22:25–29; 23:27), his birth in the cosmopolitan city of Tarsus in the Roman province of Cilicia (22:3), his Jewish name Saul (7:58), his Pharisaic education in Jerusalem (22:3), his arrest in Jerusalem (21:33), and his eventual extradition to Rome to await trial while under house arrest (27:1–28:30). Certain other information about Paul that appears in Paul's own letters, however, is missing from Acts. For example, nowhere does Acts hint at Paul's letter-writing activity.[4] Also missing

---

(Grand Rapids: Eerdmans, 2002), 40–73. See also Maria Pascuzzi, *Paul: Windows on His Thought and World* (Winona, MN: Anselm Academic, 2014), 13–65, and Daniel T. Landry with John W. Martens, *Inquiry into the New Testament: Ancient Context to Contemporary Significance* (Winona, MN: Anselm Academic, 2019), 246–60.

3. See David E. Aune, *The New Testament in Its Literary Environment*, ed. Wayne A. Meeks (Philadelphia: Westminster, 1987), 77–78. Acts shares several features that were distinctive of ancient historical writing, including the presence of an introductory preface addressed to a patron (Acts 1:1–5) and numerous speeches given by assorted characters in the narrative (2:14–36; 3:11–26; 7:1–60; 13:16–41; 17:22–31; 22:3–21; 24:10–21; 26:1–29). See Aune, *The New Testament*, 120–36.

4. Some argue that this seeming unfamiliarity with the letters of Paul can be explained on the basis that Paul's letters had not yet been widely circulated as a collection. See Martin Hengel and Anna Maria Schwemer, *Paul between Damascus and Antioch: The Unknown Years* (Louisville: Westminster John Knox, 1997), 3.

from the Acts' account of Paul's final trip to Jerusalem is any reference to the delivery of a collection taken up for the benefit of the poor in Jerusalem (see Rom. 15:25–28; 2 Cor. 9:1–5). This particular omission is striking, since in several of his letters Paul expresses how seriously he takes this undertaking, which was enjoined on him by the movement's leaders in Jerusalem (see Gal. 2:10).[5] Also missing from the otherwise detailed account in Acts of Paul's three missionary journeys (Acts 13:4–14:24; 15:36–18:17; 18:23–20:38) is any apparent awareness of the sojourn in Arabia that Paul mentions in his Letter to the Galatians (Gal. 1:17), a period of two to three years.[6] These gaps in Acts become all the more mystifying in light of the author's seeming insinuation that he accompanied Paul for at least some of the apostle's travels (e.g., Acts 21:1; 27:1; 28:1).

Equally problematic for the task of reconstructing Paul's life are the many thematic and chronological contradictions that come into view whenever one compares the Paul of Acts with the Paul of the letters. For example, on a number of occasions in Acts Paul delivers speeches that seem to demonstrate a solid facility with the conventions of Greco-Roman rhetoric (see Acts 13:16–41; 26:1–23). In his letters, however, Paul explicitly disavows any facility with the conventions of oratory, an apparent deficiency that others also noticed (see 1 Cor. 2:1–4; 2 Cor. 10:10; 11:6). Like the Apostle Peter, Paul is frequently presented in Acts as a powerful miracle worker (Acts 14:8–11; 15:12; 16:18; 19:11–12). But only once in his letters does Paul mention having performed signs and wonders (2 Cor. 12:12).[7] As Paul tells it, he made a total of two trips to Jerusalem and planned a third (Gal. 1:18; 2:1; Rom. 15:25). By contrast, Acts has Paul visiting Jerusalem a total of five times.[8]

Another tension between Acts and the letters is of a more thematic nature, having to do with Paul's standing as a Torah-abiding Jew. While nothing in his letters suggests that Paul was anything but

5. Pascuzzi, *Paul*, 23.

6. See Joseph A. Fitzmyer, SJ, *Paul and His Theology: A Brief Sketch*, 2nd ed. (Englewood Cliffs, NJ: Prentice Hall, 1989), 5.

7. See the helpful list of examples provided by Pascuzzi, *Paul*, 23. See also Calvin Roetzel, *Paul: The Man and the Myth* (Minneapolis: Fortress, 1999), 10–11.

8. Pascuzzi, *Paul*, 36–44.

an observant Jew (see Gal. 1:14 and Phil. 3:5–6), Acts seems intent on presenting Paul not only as eminently faithful in adhering to Jewish ancestral customs but also thoroughly non-controversial in this regard (see Acts 22:3; 23:6; 24:11–17; 25:8; 26:4–5). According to the author of Acts, Paul willingly had his Gentile coworker Timothy circumcised in order to appease otherwise unknown conservative Jewish believers in Jesus (Acts 16:3). But this is at odds with what Paul says in the Letter to the Galatians where he insists that his Gentile coworker Titus was not compelled to be circumcised (Gal. 2:3). Acts also takes pains to depict Paul as someone who persevered to evangelize fellow Jews despite experiencing their habitual rejection of his proclamation. Indeed, Acts sometimes makes it appear as if Paul's efforts to evangelize Gentiles resulted as a direct consequence of such rejection (see Acts 13:46; 18:5–6; 28:25–29). This portrait of Paul in Acts as a missionary to fellow Jews is somewhat in tension, however, with the uncontested letters, which all appear to be addressed almost exclusively to Gentiles.

Finally, Acts largely depicts Paul as someone who had relatively cordial relations with fellow Jewish missionaries like himself. Several of his letters suggest, however, that Paul had significant differences of opinion over a variety of issues with other Jewish missionary figures, even including the Apostle Peter (see Gal. 2:11–14). The principal differences all seem to have dealt with the intra-Jewish debate over the kinds of requirements—in particular circumcision for males—that should be placed on Gentiles in order for them to be become authentic members of God's covenant family. As will become clear later, there were other tensions as well, including disagreements over what constituted the marks of authentic apostleship (see 2 Cor. 10:1–12:21).

The Primacy of Paul's Letters

The tendency of Acts either to downplay or gloss over such disagreements actually yields insight into one of the major purposes for which Acts may have been written. As David Aune has proposed, it appears that one of the main functions of Acts is to provide narrative "definition" and "legitimation" for a movement that, by the early second century, sorely required a stable identity. Acts promotes such definition by showing how the surprising preponderance of Gentiles within the new movement by Luke's day was guided by God's Spirit. At the same time, Acts cultivates legitimation for this comparatively new social and religious movement by highlighting its roots in the ancient Jewish faith.[9] The strong emphasis that Acts places on Paul as a pious, non-controversial Jew certainly reflects the historical reality of Paul's own essential Jewishness; at the same time, it functions as a confirmation for the reader that this new social and religious phenomenon is really not so novel after all.

The historical reality was likely more complicated than the author of Acts sometimes portrays it. Without question Paul was and remained a committed Jew who understood Jesus to be the long-awaited Jewish Messiah sent in fulfillment of what Paul took to be the promises foretold in the Jewish Scriptures.[10] This latter point bears repeating, since many regard Paul as someone who repudiated his native Judaism. Despite his enduring Jewishness, however, Paul remained a controversial figure for many of his contemporaries, both Jewish and non-Jewish alike.[11]

When faced with these kinds of contradictions and discrepancies that arise in the comparison between the Paul of Acts and the Paul of the letters, many scholars point to the fact that Acts is a third-person account written as many as fifty to seventy years after the events it purports to describe, perhaps even longer. The author of Acts, in other words, was not an eyewitness to the events described

---

9. Aune, *The New Testament*, 137–38.

10. It is not correct to think of Paul as someone who repudiated his Jewish ancestral customs as part of his commitment to Christ. Nor is it accurate to envision either Paul or the members of his communities as "Christians." See Mark D. Nanos, "A Jewish View," in *Four Views on the Apostle Paul*, ed. Stanley N. Gundry and Michael F. Bird (Grand Rapids: Zondervan, 2012), 167.

11. Something of the controversial Paul is seen in the following passage: "You see, brother, how many thousands of believers there are among the Jews, and they are all zealous for the law. They have been told about you that you teach all the Jews living among the Gentiles to forsake Moses, and that you tell them not to circumcise their children or observe the customs" (Acts 21:20–21). Both the letters of Paul and the book of Acts testify to the provocative nature of Paul's message and ministry both to insiders and outsiders (see 16:20–24; 17:6–9; 2 Cor. 11:24–26). As Michael F. Bird notes about Paul, "You do not get beaten, flogged, imprisoned, and stoned without saying and doing things that are deemed controversial, offensive, and even subversive." See Bird, *Four Views*, 9.

in his narrative. Indeed, if recent scholarly proposals are correct that argue that Acts dates to the early second century, this would mean that Acts was written certainly by a second- or perhaps even a third-generation believer.[12] By contrast, the seven uncontested letters of Paul were likely written within a seven- to ten-year time period, spanning the years 50–60 CE, and are therefore chronologically earlier sources as well as first-person accounts.

While it should be recognized, of course, that Paul's own agendas shape both his view of himself and of the events he describes, sources that are chronologically earlier and contain first-hand accounts should as a general rule be preferred over chronologically later third-person accounts.[13] This does not mean, however, that Acts should be discredited as having no historical value. Without Acts, it is almost impossible to develop a sketch of the historical Paul at all.[14] Indeed, one could argue that on many substantive historical issues pertaining to Paul both Acts and the letters are mutually supportive. For example, both sources confirm—though with varying detail—that prior to his commitment to Christ Paul was a persecutor of early Jewish Jesus believers (see Acts 8:1–3; 9:1–2; 1 Cor. 15:9; Gal. 1:13). Similarly, both sources highlight the foundational role that Paul's encounter with the risen Jesus had for his own vocational understanding (see Acts 22:6–21; Gal. 1:15–16). Nonetheless, owing to such factors as the chronological observations noted above, an awareness of the literary conventions of ancient historiography, and above all the legitimating purposes for which Acts was written, it is important to recognize that Acts is oftentimes quite selective and compressed in its general portrayal of the development of primitive Christianity and in its portrait of Paul.[15]

The remainder of this study will touch on those aspects of the historical Paul that have particular relevance for illuminating the topics of religious experience and common life that are the focus of this book. While these historical observations will be based, for the

---

12. See Paula Fredriksen, *Paul: The Pagans' Apostle* (New Haven: Yale University Press, 2017), 170.

13. See Fredriksen, *Paul*, 62.

14. Jürgen Becker, *Paul: Apostle to the Gentiles*, trans. O. C. Dean Jr. (Louisville: John Knox, 1993), 16.

15. Raymond Brown, *Introduction to the New Testament*, Anchor Bible Reference Library (New York: Doubleday, 1997), 320-22.

Approximate Time Line of Paul's Life

4–6 BCE	Birth of Paul likely in Tarsus of Cilicia (modern day Turkey)
30 CE	Crucifixion of Jesus of Nazareth
33/34 CE	Paul's experience of an encounter with the risen Jesus
33/34–36 CE	Missionary activity in Arabia (mentioned by Paul in his letters but not by Acts)
36 CE	First visit to Jerusalem
36–49 CE	Paul's first missionary journey as reported in the book of Acts. A second visit to Jerusalem in 49 CE.
49–52 CE	Paul's second missionary journey as reported in Acts. The founding of church communities in Philippi, Thessalonica, and Corinth. First Thessalonians likely written from Corinth around the year 50.
53–57 CE	Paul's third missionary journey as reported in Acts. The founding of the church community in Galatia. First and (parts of) Second Corinthians written, as well as Galatians, Philippians, and Philemon.
58 CE	Journey to Jerusalem to deliver aid to the poor; arrest/imprisonment. According to Acts Paul appeals as a Roman citizen to be tried in Rome. Romans, likely Paul's last letter, written around the year 58.
59–60 CE	Arrival in Rome and placement under house arrest (Acts ends here).
62–64 CE	Executed during the reign of Roman emperor Nero. The account of Paul being beheaded found in later Christian traditions may be a legend. He did, however, likely suffer a violent death, much as Jesus did.

most part, on the evidence of Paul's letters, they will also draw attention when appropriate to those instances where Acts either confirms or lends support to what can be gathered in Paul's letters. Particular emphasis will be given to the following two areas that are crucial for understanding not only the life and mission of Paul but his religious sensibilities: (1) his pastoral activity as a shaper of communal behavior and identity, and (2) Paul's universalistic vision concerning what the God of Israel had in store for both Jews and Gentiles at the end of time, a time that Paul thought to be fast approaching.

Methodological Observations on the Nature of Paul's Letters: The Lens of First Thessalonians

Although not listed first among the thirteen letters attributed to the Apostle Paul in the New Testament, the letter called 1 Thessalonians is in all probability the earliest surviving letter of Paul.[16] Written perhaps as early as only twenty years after the events of Jesus' execution (thirty to thirty-three CE), 1 Thessalonians provides a helpful index both for how Paul conceived of his own vocation and how the received message about the death and resurrection of Jesus affected the lives of some of the earliest believers in the Gospel proclamation.

In an effort to help guide the reader in the navigation of 1 Thessalonians, as well as Paul's correspondence more generally, several observations on issues related both to content and methodology should be addressed from the start. First, it is important to remember that Paul did not write his letters to provide an extended narrative account of the words and deeds of Jesus such as we find in the Gospels. The miraculous activity associated with Jesus, his teaching in parables, the detailed accounts of Jesus' final days, the dramatic accounts of the empty tomb, and the vividly described resurrection appearances of Jesus are nowhere to be found in Paul's letters. In part, these omissions can be explained in terms of considerations related

---

16. It is impossible to know for certain, however, whether 1 Thessalonians was the earliest letter written by Paul. The seven uncontested letters of Paul (Romans, 1 and 2 Corinthians, Galatians, Philippians, Philemon, and 1 Thessalonians) roughly all date between the years of 50 CE to 58 CE. Since Paul's active years of ministry likely spanned some thirty years (33 to 64 CE), it is very possible that he wrote letters even earlier than 1 Thessalonians—letters that, unfortunately, no longer survive.

to chronology. All of Paul's letters were written within a period that predates the first written Gospel, the Gospel of Mark, by some twenty years. Indeed, during the likely thirty-year-long active ministry of Paul (33 CE to 64 CE) the bulk of the material now found in the New Testament Gospels was still being transmitted primarily orally. This does not mean that Paul was necessarily unaware of some (many?) of the stories and traditions that eventually found their way into the written Gospels. Indeed, scattered references in the uncontested letters seem to point to a strong familiarity on Paul's part with the events associated especially with Jesus' final days.[17]

Issues of chronology represent, however, only part of the story when accounting for the absence of anything like a sustained Gospel narrative in Paul's letters; Paul's very theological center of gravity is markedly different from what we encounter in the Gospels. Paul is less interested in replicating a chronological account of Jesus' ministry than with placing before his readers the overall pattern of Jesus' life in order to have it serve as the pattern for their own lives.[18] This shift in emphasis helps to explain those places in Paul's letters where the apostle encourages his audience to reorient their attitudes and behavior in accordance with what Paul calls the "mind of Christ" (1 Cor. 2:16; Phil. 2:5). To have the mind of Christ or to think like Christ amounts essentially to living a life where desire for control over others and seeking the esteem of others is turned on its head in favor of self-sacrificial regard for the well-being of the other person and of the community. The attitude is summed up brilliantly in Paul's invitation to the community resident in the Roman colony of Philippi to transform their understanding of communal fellowship: "Do nothing from selfish ambition or conceit, but in humility regard others as better than yourselves. Let each of you look not to your own interests, but to the interests of others. Let the same mind be in you that was in Christ Jesus" (Phil. 2:3–5). This passage sounds remarkably similar to Jesus' challenge to the disciples as preserved in Mark's Gospel: "You know that among the Gentiles those whom they recognize as their rulers lord it over them, and their great ones are tyrants

---

17. See Rom. 15:3; 1 Cor. 15:3–4; Phil. 2:7–8. Paul is also aware of Jesus' strict prohibition of divorce (1 Cor. 7:10–11).

18. Luke T. Johnson, *The Real Jesus: The Misguided Quest for the Historical Jesus and the Truth of the Traditional Gospels* (San Francisco: Harper, 1998), 119.

over them. But it is not so among you; but whoever wishes to become great among you must be your servant, and whoever wishes to be first among you must be slave of all" (Mark 10:42–44). It is typical of Paul that he records the substance of Jesus' manner of living, rather than the precise sayings and individual deeds of Jesus.

Second, any examination of Paul's letters should recognize the occasional, issue-specific nature of Paul's correspondence. Despite the fact that a significant amount of theological reflection is contained in Paul's writings, his letters should not be viewed as abstract, timeless pieces of theological doctrine; instead, the letters are best conceived of as "words on target."[19] Put another way, the letters of Paul consistently engage with the questions and actual lived experiences of the persons who constituted the members of the communities first addressed by Paul's letters. As a founder and shaper of small cells of believers located in the major urban centers of the Mediterranean world, Paul employed letters to function as surrogates or substitutes for his personal presence.[20]

A recognition of the situational character of Paul's letters makes their study not only interesting and timely but challenging as well. While it is sometimes relatively easy to see the places where Paul is engaging the questions and experiences of his communities (see 1 Cor. 7:1–40), Paul's responses to these matters often remain far from clear. Moreover, there are also many places in Paul's letters where the precise issue at hand is itself unclear. Both factors have a bearing on how one should think of the formal character of Paul's correspondence. In additional to being occasional, the letters unfortunately preserve, for the most part, the interaction of Paul alone. That is, we only see the questions, issues, and experiences of his communities as these are refracted through the medium of Paul's own words, interpretations, sensibilities, and personal experience. No less than with the interpretation of the Gospels, any interpretation of Paul's letters will invariably be limited in terms of its outcomes.

---

19. See also Jürgen Becker, *Paul the Apostle: The Triumph of God in Life and Thought* (Philadelphia: Fortress, 1984), 62–63.

20. Leander E. Keck, *Paul and His Letters*, ed. Gerhard Krodel, 2nd ed., rev. and enlarged, Proclamation Commentaries (Philadelphia: Fortress, 1988), 20–21. See also Becker, *Paul: Apostle to the Gentiles*, 7.

The Significance of Paul's Understanding of His Vocation as Apostle to the Gentiles

Unlike Jesus, who as far as we know seems to have confined his ministry to fellow Jews living in the villages of rural Galilee, Paul of Tarsus directed his proclamation concerning the death and resurrection of Jesus primarily to non-Jews who lived in the major urban centers of the Greco-Roman world.[21] Paul's focus on Gentiles stems directly from his own transformative religious experience of having encountered the risen Jesus (see 1 Cor. 9:1; 15:8). Paul speaks most explicitly to this event in his Letter to the Galatians:

> But when God, who had set me apart before I was born and called me through his grace, was please to reveal his Son to me, so that I might proclaim him among the Gentiles, I did not confer with any human being, nor did I go up to Jerusalem to those who were already apostles before me, but I went away at once into Arabia, and afterwards I returned to Damascus. (Gal. 1:15–17)

Paul's own account of this event contrasts sharply with the significantly more detailed versions of this episode that are found in the book of Acts (see Acts 9:3–9; 22:6–11; 26:12–18). Whereas the emphasis in Acts is on highly dramatic visual and auditory phenomena that literally accost Paul physically, Paul himself speaks to an experience that appears more subtle, if just as transformative.[22] Depending on how one translates a single preposition in Greek (*en*), Paul's meaning might better be expressed as that God's Son was revealed "in me," and not "to me" (Gal. 1:16). However one might interpret what must have been a deeply personal religious experience for Paul, the text seems clear enough in its witness to the significance that this revelation of the risen Jesus had for Paul's understanding of

---

21. The stories in the Gospels of Jesus interacting with Gentiles are few in number and reflect the situation of later decades when non-Jews constituted the dominant demographic of early Christianity. That is, this phenomenon of the Gentile mission that was well under way during the period of the composition of the Gospels is read back into the stories of Jesus' ministry.

22. Despite differences in the three retellings of this episode, each account in Acts speaks of Paul falling on the ground as a result of seeing and hearing a powerful revelation.

his sense of vocation. Before his encounter with the risen Jesus, Paul admits to persecuting fellow Jews as a result of their public testimony about Jesus being the long-awaited Jewish Messiah.[23] Now, as a result of this same encounter with the risen Christ, Paul recognizes a new commission to proclaim the Gospel of the risen Messiah to the Gentiles (Gal. 1:16).

Paul seems to have interpreted this encounter primarily against the backdrop of Jewish scriptural terminology pertaining to the call of a prophet (see Isa. 49:1–6; Jer. 1:5), those figures who in Israel's past served as spokespersons for God. As Krister Stendahl argued some time ago, Paul did not undergo a conversion to a new religion, nor much less a transition away from a sinful to a righteous life.[24] Rather, the still Jewish and law-observant Paul came to a renewed sense of how best to live his life as a Jew who was and remained always devoted to the God of Israel. As noted by Stendahl, Paul is the recipient in this encounter of a surprising "assignment" to bring the knowledge of the Gospel, as well as the mysterious plan of the God of Israel for the future of all humanity, to the larger Gentile world.[25] Paul was, in other words, "called," as opposed to "converted."

Religious Experience and Common Life: Apocalypticism and Identity Formation in First Thessalonians

While it is possible that Jews comprised some portion of the community membership in the city of Thessalonica (see Acts 17:4–6),

---

23. Both the book of Acts and the letters mutually confirm the memory that Paul persecuted early Jesus believers (Acts 8:1–3; 9:1–2, 13, 21; 22:4–5; 26:9–11; 1 Cor. 15:9; Gal. 1:13; Phil. 3:6). It is not at all clear, however, what precisely this persecution entailed or even why Paul engaged in it. For a helpful synopsis of the different scholarly explanations on this issue, see Fredriksen, *Paul*, 77–93. Fredriksen is probably correct in her assumption that some of the more traditional explanations given for this episode in Paul's life are not, in the end, persuasive. For example, there is no evidence to confirm the contention found in both popular and scholarly circles that first-century Jews would have found the message of a Messiah who was crucified as somehow contrary to Torah or inherently offensive to the God of Israel. See Fedriksen, *Paul*, 83–84.

24. Krister Stendahl, *Paul among Jews and Gentiles and Other Essays* (Minneapolis: Fortress, 1976), 7–12.

25. Stendahl, *Paul among Jews and Gentiles*, 7.

the nucleus of the assembly appears to have been non-Jews.[26] Note, for example, Paul's remarks in the thanksgiving section of 1 Thessalonians:[27]

> For the people of those regions report about us what kind of welcome we had among you, and how you turned to God from idols, to serve a living and true God, and to wait for his Son from heaven, who he raised from the dead—Jesus, who rescues us from the wrath that is coming. (1 Thess. 1:9–10)

Since it was well known that Jews disavowed the visible representation of the God of Israel in any form whatsoever (see Exod. 20:4–5), Paul's reference to idols in this passage can only mean that Paul is referring to a non-Jewish implied reader. These Gentiles "turned to God from idols, to serve a living and true God" (1 Thess. 1:9). This passage powerfully conveys Paul's self-definition as a Jew who regards the deities worshiped by the majority Greco-Roman culture as illegitimate in comparison to the God of Israel. At the same time, these verses function to evoke the initial call experience of Paul's Gentile audience, an experience that Paul reminds them entailed their repudiation of their ancestral religious customs and the attendant transferal of their loyalties to the God of Israel. As will be seen in more detail below, such behavior was not only rare; it was also socially and religiously disruptive.

This passage also illustrates an important facet of the religious experience that Paul and his community share, namely, that they find themselves living in the tensive moment between the death and

---

26. As Fedriksen has recently observed, this does not mean that Paul was uninterested in the salvation or fate of Israel. Indeed, Paul seems to have seen the salvation of Gentiles as integral to what he understood to be the irrevocable commitment of the God of Israel to the covenant people, namely, the Jewish people. See Fredriksen, *Paul*, 166.

27. Ancient letters tended to adhere to a stereotypical format. Ordinarily the correspondence opened with the inclusion of what was called a *prescript* or salutation, which included the following three pieces of information: name of the sender, name of the addressee, and a simple greeting. Immediately after came the section called a thanksgiving. Quite often this section simply expressed a wish for the addressee's health. Paul's prescripts and especially his thanksgivings—Galatians being an exception—tend to be much more elaborate than the many examples of ordinary letters preserved from this time period. See Roetzel, *The Letters*, 51–66.

resurrection of Jesus and the expectation of his imminent return (1 Thess. 1:10; 4:15–18; 5:2). Like Jesus, Paul was a Jew whose outlook on the world was shaped by profoundly apocalyptic categories of thinking. Apocalypticism is difficult to define, however; the term is used by scholars both to identify a particular genre of writing popular in Jewish and Christian circles in the Second Temple period and to refer to a distinctive way of viewing reality.

While the book of Revelation is the only full-blown apocalyptic writing found in the New Testament, evidence of apocalyptic thinking can be found throughout many New Testament texts. The term itself literally translates as an "unveiling" or "revealing." Whether applied to an entire text or to a pattern of thinking, what is revealed or unveiled is typically considered to be of ultimate, even cosmic significance. One would not go too far afield to say that what is of ultimate, cosmic significance for Paul is the apocalyptic event of the cross and resurrection of Christ. As Paul himself notes in several places in his letters, this event has profoundly transformed his experience of himself and of his relationship to the world: "I have been crucified with Christ; and it is no longer I who live, but it is Christ who lives in me. And the life I now live in the flesh I live by faith in the Son of God, who loved me and gave himself for me" (Gal. 2:19–20). Much of what will follow in the remaining chapters of this study will be devoted to exploring the influence that the event of the cross and resurrection had for shaping Paul's reflections on the kind of common life that he sees as being in conformity with this apocalyptic event.

The apocalyptic perspective includes the following more or less stable features: (1) an expectation that in the imminent future God will act in some decisive manner to address injustice and sin in the world; (2) the belief that events on earth are shaped and influenced by cosmic forces, including especially forces of evil; and (3) the belief that those who constitute God's righteous ones will be vindicated at the close of the age when God or God's agent judges the world. As this list indicates, the apocalyptic perspective tended to be sharply dualistic and attentive to end-time events.[28] One of these end-time events, the resurrection of the dead, functioned for certain Jewish groups like the Pharisees—a group to which Paul himself belonged

---

28. See Pascuzzi, *Paul*, 93–101.

(Acts 23:6; 26:5; Phil. 3:5)—as a distinguishing feature of the end time. Attested in such texts as the book of Daniel in the Jewish canon and the deutero-canonical book called 2 Maccabees, the resurrection of God's righteous, who were often depicted as suffering on account of their fidelity to God, became the quintessential symbol of God finally bringing all things to an end. While the majority of Paul's Jewish contemporaries saw the matter otherwise, Paul became convinced that the end time event of the resurrection had been realized in the resurrection of a single individual, Jesus of Nazareth. And very soon, Paul believed, the collective resurrection of the people of God would follow at the return of Jesus. While there is no record of what Paul actually proclaimed in Thessalonica at the time he founded the community, indications in the letter suggest that the announcement of Jesus' imminent arrival at the close of the age occupied an important place both in Paul's initial preaching and his subsequent pastoral advice to the community (1 Thess. 1:10; 3:13; 5:2).

The apocalyptic atmosphere that informs 1 Thessalonians is also likely related to the social reality on the ground at the time of Paul's writing. Multiple passages in the letter allude to the experience of persecution borne by members of the assembly (1 Thess. 1:6; 2:14; 3:3). Despite popular perceptions to the contrary, there is little evidence of empire-wide persecution of Christians by Roman imperial authorities until the third century CE. Prior to this time, by far the more typical form of distress experienced by the first Christians consisted of popular societal scorn.[29] As a consequence of their conversion, new converts were perceived by their contemporaries as social and religious deviants. The reason for this was simple. To the minds of many in the dominant Greco-Roman culture, to not attend to the worship of the gods through formal prayer and sacrifice was to run the risk of provoking divine retribution on the community as a whole. And since religious piety was tied so closely to family values and civic virtue, a convert risked being labeled as a dishonorable person, hence worthy of shaming. Paul's awareness of persecution in the form of societal scorn goes a long way to explaining the gentle, encouraging tone of the letter (1:8; 2:8, 19) as well as his clear affirmation to the

---

29. See Candida Moss, *The Myth of Persecution: How Early Christians Invented a Story of Martyrdom* (New York: HarperOne, 2014).

community of the glorious destiny awaiting them (1:10; 3:13; 5:4–9). At a time when all the members of the first Christian assemblies were first-generation Christians, Paul recognizes that the psychic pain attendant upon being recipients of deviancy labeling from the surrounding culture could potentially result in defections back to the social and religious status quo.

At the center of Paul's apocalyptic conviction is his belief that the same Jesus who was resurrected from the dead would soon return to inaugurate a new age. So confident is Paul concerning this expectation that he places before the community a vision of what this end time event might entail. To do this he employs stereotypical apocalyptic imagery taken from the symbolic world of both the Jewish Scriptures and Second Temple apocalyptic thought more generally:

> For this we declare to you by the word of the Lord, that we who are alive, who are left until the coming of the Lord, will by no means precede those who have died. For the Lord himself, with a cry of command, with the archangel's call and with the sound of God's trumpet, will descend from heaven, and the dead in Christ will rise first. Then we who are alive, who are left, will be caught up in the clouds together with them to meet the Lord in the air; and so we will be with the Lord forever. (1 Thess. 4:15–17)

The presenting issue in the community that prompts Paul to describe this event seems to have been related to an anxiety over community members who had died sometime after the founding of the church. Whether fed by pessimistic attitudes concerning the possibility of an afterlife or by Paul's own impassioned convictions about the shortness of time left before the close of the age, a crisis had emerged that had led to grieving and loss of hope (1 Thess. 4:13). Paul's version of the sequence of end-time events is certainly vivid and dramatic. At the same time, certain details remain ambiguous. For example, it is unclear from Paul's comments precisely where the new age will be located; will it be in heaven in the clouds or on a renewed earthly paradise? A somewhat similar ambiguity is found a little later after this passage where Paul displays a reluctance to provide any sort of definite timetable for the events associated with the close of the age (see 5:1–3). What does seem clear, however, is Paul's overriding pastoral concern to assure the community that nothing, not even death, will dissolve their bonds of fellowship both to one another and to Jesus. Whatever the close of the age will be like and wherever it will be located, it will be defined by the communal experience of enduring fellowship with one another and with Jesus (4:17).

Stated another way, Paul's confidence in the imminent return of the resurrected Jesus is wedded to issues of common life. And while in this particular passage the focus is on common life in the age to come, Paul is mainly concerned throughout 1 Thessalonians with how the community might live out their destiny in their very ordinary daily lives in the present: "For God has destined us not for wrath but for obtaining salvation through our Lord Jesus Christ, who died for us, so that whether we are awake or asleep we may live with him" (1 Thess. 5:9–10). Although Paul is certain of the reality of a glorious afterlife, the true center of gravity in his thought is on life in community in this world. Paul understood life in Christ to be not just a future hope, but a possibility right now that could be embodied in lives of transformed thinking and behavior. This conviction is what lies behind the highly metaphorical language Paul employs near the end of the letter where he designates the members of the community as children of the day and children of the light (5:5). The imagery is symbolic of ethical renewal. Other suggestive examples of Paul's focus on transformation appear throughout the text of 1 Thessalonians: Paul's summons to abstain from sexual immorality (4:1–8), his invitation to forego retaliation for evil (5:15), as well as his implicit invitation to the community to reevaluate their culturally inherited outlook on death as a final ending from which there can never be a hope for a new beginning (4:13–14). This dynamic pattern of living out in ordinary life the implications of the cross and resurrection of Jesus will be the focus of the remaining chapters of this study.

Summary

Paul understood his vocation as the Apostle to the Gentiles as that of bringing the Gospel proclamation of the crucified and raised Jesus to a predominantly non-Jewish audience. Paul undertook this mission as a fully committed Jew who believed that the God of Israel was at work in the life, death, and resurrection of the Jewish Messiah, Jesus.

Paul's message was framed in the apocalyptic categories native to his contemporary Judaism. These categories were adapted, however, to align with Paul's overwhelming experience of having encountered the living Christ in the cosmos-altering events of the death and resurrection of Jesus. Paul saw his mission as one not simply of converting Gentiles from their native polytheistic beliefs, but of actively shaping them into communities marked by renewed patterns of thinking and behavior that distinguished them from their surrounding culture.

Questions for Review

1. What reasons prompt scholars to employ Acts of the Apostles cautiously when reconstructing the Paul of history?
2. What is meant by the term "occasional" as applied to Paul's letters?
3. What are the main features of the apocalyptic perspective that one sees on display in Paul's letters?

Questions for Reflection

1. Does the fact that the Paul of Acts and the Paul of the letters are so different from one another affect their value as historical resources in your assessment? If so, in what sense?
2. How does an appreciation for the situational character of Paul's correspondence help us to interpret what Paul was trying to accomplish with his letters?
3. What difference does it make if one views the experience of Paul's encounter with Christ as a prophetic call and not a conversion experience?

For Further Reading

Aune, David E. *The New Testament in Its Literary Environment.* Edited by Wayne A. Meeks. Philadelphia: Westminster, 1987.

Becker, Jürgen. *Paul: Apostle to the Gentiles.* Translated by O. C. Dean Jr. Louisville: John Knox, 1993.

———. *Paul the Apostle: The Triumph of God in Life and Thought.* Philadelphia: Fortress, 1984.

Brown, Raymond. *Introduction to the New Testament*. Anchor Bible Reference Library. New York: Doubleday, 1997.

Fitzmyer, Joseph A., SJ. *Paul and His Theology: A Brief Sketch*. 2nd ed. New Jersey: Prentice Hall, 1989.

Fredriksen, Paula. *Paul: The Pagans' Apostle*. New Haven: Yale University Press, 2017.

Hengel, Martin, and Anna Maria Schwemer. *Paul between Damascus and Antioch: The Unknown Years*. Louisville: Westminster John Knox, 1997.

Johnson, Luke T. *The Real Jesus: The Misguided Quest for the Historical Jesus and the Truth of the Traditional Gospels*. San Francisco: Harper, 1996.

Landry, David T., and John W. Mertens. *Inquiry into the New Testament: Ancient Context to Contemporary Significance*. Winona, MN: Anselm Academic, 2019.

Leander E. Keck. *Paul and His Letters*. Edited by Gerhard Krodel. 2nd ed., revised and enlarged. Proclamation Commentaries. Philadelphia: Fortress, 1988.

Moss, Candida. T*he Myth of Persecution: How Early Christians Invented a Story of Martyrdom*, New York: HarperOne, 2014.

Pascuzzi, Maria. *Paul: Windows on His Thought and World*. Winona, MN: Anselm Academic, 2014.

Roetzel, Calvin. *Paul: The Man and the Myth*. Minneapolis: Fortress, 1999.

Stendahl, Krister. *Paul among Jews and Gentiles and Other Essays*. Minneapolis: Fortress, 1976.

7

Religious Experience and Common Life in the Letters of Paul

Participation in Christ and Ethical Transformation

n the previous chapter it was noted that Paul contemplated the events of the death and resurrection of Jesus from within the framework of Jewish apocalyptic categories of thought. That is to say, Paul regarded the death and resurrection of Jesus as a cosmos-altering event that had revealed in a definitive way the power of God. Paul expresses this conviction to the Christian assembly residing in the city of Rome in what may have been the last letter he ever wrote: "I am not ashamed of the gospel; it is the power of God for salvation to everyone who has faith, to the Jew first and also to the Greek" (Rom. 1:16).[1] In an ancient setting where the claims of the

---

1. Given the complexity involved in fixing the chronology of Paul's letters, it is impossible to establish with certainty which of the uncontested letters was the last that Paul wrote. If the reference to the *praetorium* found in Phil. 1:13 refers to Rome—itself uncertain—then it is possible to see Philippians as the final or one of the final letters Paul wrote. My judgment that Romans was likely Paul's final letter is informed by the recent work of Gregory Tatum on the topic of the relative chronology of Paul's career. See Gregory Tatum, OP, *New Chapters in the Life of Paul: The Relative Chronology of His Career*, Catholic Biblical Quarterly Monograph Series 41 (Washington, DC: Catholic Biblical Association, 2006).

first Christians were rejected or ridiculed by many, Paul responds by embracing the paradoxical power displayed in the seemingly power-less circumstances of Jesus' execution.

This chapter will analyze Paul's understanding of the nature of this power and explore how Paul conceives of this power as hav-ing the potential to shape the common life of the assemblies that he founded. The results of this analysis will show that Paul reflects on this power in accordance with a more comprehensive conceptual model of participation in Christ. For Paul the religious experience of such participation both enables and empowers communal and individual ethical transformation. The Letter to the Philippians, the Letter to Philemon, and the Letter to the Galatians will serve as the basis upon which the claims of this chapter will depend.

The Letter to the Philippians: Imprisonment in Light of Paul's Ultimate Concern

The immediate occasion for Paul writing to the Philippians was his personal misfortune in consequence of proclaiming the Gospel. Paul writes from what appears to be a situation of house arrest. Students often express surprise that Paul exhibits a hopeful, even positive atti-tude to his situation of imprisonment (Phil. 1:18–19). Admittedly, this does seem strange, especially when one considers that Paul seems aware that he could be facing his own imminent execution (1:20). Paul's confident attitude likely bears some connection to his concern over how the Philippians may be processing what had happened to him. Any number of distressing questions might have arisen in the assembly in response to the circumstances of Paul's arrest: Why was Paul arrested? What does it say about us that we committed ourselves to someone who is now imprisoned? Will we ever see Paul again? The latter question, in particular, likely entered the minds of many in the community, a question perhaps all the more painful to contemplate in light of their own ongoing experience of persecution (see 1:27–30).

Both in our own culture as well as in the ancient world, incar-ceration brought with it the potential for the verdict of shame (Phil. 1:20).[2] Much as Martin Luther King Jr. used his letter from a

_____

2. Dennis Hamm, SJ, *Philippians, Colossians, Philemon*, Catholic Commentary on Sacred Scriptures (Grand Rapids: Baker, 2013), 85.

Birmingham jail to contextualize his own imprisonment against the background of the ultimate value of the civil rights movement, Paul makes it clear to the community that his imprisonment flows out of a vocation both to preach and advance the Gospel (1:12–13, 16). Embracing the Gospel as his ultimate concern, Paul challenges the community in Philippi to reimagine the categories of what is considered truly honorable.[3] At the same time, whatever his actual outlook was concerning the possibility of either his execution or acquittal (1:22–24), Paul makes certain to assure the assembly in Philippi that he is confident that he will see them again (1:25–26).

Religious Experience as Participation in Christ

Paul also uses the occasion of his imprisonment to communicate to the assembly his reflections on his own religious experience. A fundamental aspect of that experience is his consciousness of participating in Christ: "It is my eager expectation and hope that I will not be put to shame in any way, but that by speaking with all boldness, Christ will be exalted now as always in my body, whether by life or by death. For to me, living is Christ and dying is gain" (Phil. 1:20–21). Throughout his letters Paul frequently describes salvation as having to do with the experiential conviction of union with Christ (see Rom. 8:10; 2 Cor. 5:17; 13:5; Gal. 2:19–20; 3:27–28; Phil. 3:8–9).[4] Paul understands such union as an experience made possible as a result of the exalted status of the resurrected Jesus, whom Paul believes is now alive in a new way (Phil. 2:9).

To be clear, Paul does not say that he presently shares in the exalted resurrection life of Jesus. Indeed, as he notes a little later in the letter, such a glorious existence is a future goal: "Not that I have already obtained this or have already reached the goal; but I press on to make it my own, because Christ Jesus has made me his own"

---

3. For the importance of the categories of shame and honor in ancient Mediterranean society, see Maria Pascuzzi, *Paul: Windows on His Thought and World* (Winona, MN: Anselm Academic, 2014), 237.

4. See the discussion of this theme in James D. G. Dunn, *The Theology of Paul the Apostle* (Grand Rapids: Eerdmans, 1998), 396–401. See also Alan F. Segal, *Paul the Convert: The Apostolate and Apostasy of Saul the Pharisee* (New Haven: Yale University Press, 1990), 34–35, and Jouette M. Bassler, *Navigating Paul: An Introduction to Key Theological Concepts* (Louisville: Westminster John Knox, 2007), 35–47.

(Phil. 3:12). At the same time, Paul is adamant that his life is wholly influenced and defined by this relationship with Christ. A similar idea is expressed in the Letter to the Galatians where Paul writes, "It is no longer I who live, but it is Christ who lives in me" (Gal. 2:20). Commenting on this motif of participation, Leander Keck proposes that Paul thinks of the resurrected Jesus as a sphere of power that is both corporate and inclusive in nature.[5] Through the gift of God's Spirit, the community is empowered to live in Christ both individually and collectively. As we will see in the next chapter, Paul explores this idea most fully in his Letter to the Corinthians where he refers to the community in the following way: "Now you are the body of Christ and individually members of it" (1 Cor. 12:27; see also 10:16 and 11:29). The same pattern of thinking underlies other metaphors Paul employs to reflect on the salvation he believes to be found in Christ. In Galatians, for example, Paul describes the community as adopted children of God, who have the status of children precisely because the Spirit of the resurrected Jesus dwells in them (Gal. 4:6–7). Admittedly, this way of thinking seems alien to our contemporary sensibilities, since it assumes that there exists a transcendent dimension to reality that is as real as anything else we encounter in our lives. It also illustrates an assumption, no longer taken for granted, that we primarily are defined as persons not by ourselves but by whom we are related to.[6]

The Ethical Dimension of Participation in Christ

The most distinctive feature of Paul's notion of participation, however, concerns the ethical application that he draws from it. Evaluating his fate from the experience of his mystical encounter with Christ, Paul accepts whatever his uncertain fate might be, whether execution or acquittal. Just as importantly, this same experience empowers him to discern what would be the better outcome of the two. Although death would paradoxically entail a deepening of the experience of encounter with Jesus (Phil. 1:23), Paul ultimately sees

---

5. Leander E. Keck, *Paul and His Letters*, ed. Gerhard Krodel, 2nd ed., Proclamation Commentaries (Philadelphia: Fortress, 1988), 56.

6. Keck, *Paul*, 76.

the prospect of remaining in the world to be the better outcome. The reason for this is because such an outcome will mean the continuation of his pastoral care for the Philippian assembly (1:25–26). In other words, Paul's experience of sharing the life of Christ is what guides his prioritization of the greater good of common life and the minimization of his own personal sense of fulfillment. As Paul will go on to explain, this is also the pattern that informed the life and ministry of Jesus.

Paul continues his emphasis on the ethical life in the remainder of chapter 1 by turning attention away from himself to the behavior of the Philippian assembly more generally. Specifically, Paul encourages them, "Live your life in a manner worthy of the gospel of Christ" (Phil. 1:27). The English translation of this verse found in the NRSV unfortunately misses the fuller political resonance of the Greek verb *politeuomai* that Paul employs here. "Conduct yourself as a citizen" better approximates Paul's larger point than "live your life." Addressing an audience comprised of some who held the privileged status of Roman citizenship, Paul invites both Roman citizen and Roman non-citizen alike to pursue honor in a life defined by behaviors that embody the gospel, behaviors that Paul will clarify in the next chapter of the letter. Paul reiterates this injunction somewhat later in the letter when he identifies the community's heavenly citizenship as its defining one (3:20). It is possible to see in both these passages either a critique of Roman power or at the very least evidence of Paul's recognition that some in the assembly are being labelled as politically deviant by their neighbors.[7] Whichever is the case, Paul's deeper concern lies in inviting the community to prioritize in their common life a different order of community-enhancing values that owe their existence to an event of apocalyptic significance: the life, death, and resurrection of Jesus.

Paul clarifies the nature of these values:

> If then there is any encouragement in Christ, any consolation from love, any sharing in the Spirit, any compassion and sympathy, make my joy complete: be of the same

7. See Pascuzzi, *Paul*, 247–59. See also Michael Gorman, *Apostle of the Crucified Lord* (Grand Rapids: Eerdmans, 2002), 429–31, and Charles B. Cousar, *Philippians and Philemon*, New Testament Library (Westminster: John Knox, 2009), 44–47.

> mind, having the same love, being in full accord and of one
> mind. Do nothing from selfish ambition or conceit, but in
> humility regard others as better than yourselves. Let each
> of you look not to your own interests, but to the interests
> of others. Let the same mind be in you that was in Christ
> Jesus. (Phil. 2:1–5)

In these reflections on common life, Paul reckons honestly with the fact that communal fellowship is characterized more often than not by patterns of dysfunctionality. Accompanying the general elusiveness of communal accord are various self-serving attitudes that subtly denigrate others. Principal in this regard are attitudes of rivalry and competitive comparison, attitudes that Paul labels elsewhere as fleshly behavior (1 Cor. 3:3–4; Gal. 5:19–20). As a safeguard against the tendency to minimize the worth and value of others, Paul urges the assembly to embody an ethic of radical regard for others. Animating Paul's thinking on this issue is his recognition of the ease with which persons tend to enhance themselves at the expense of others, even others with whom they share communal ties as a result of shared commitments. What is also intriguing about Paul's advice is the way he grounds this ethic in a model of participation in what he describes as the mind of Christ (Phil. 2:5).

The Christ Hymn: Common Life as the Expression of Having the Mind of Christ

What follows next is a highly compressed recital of events recalling the public ministry of Jesus. The rhythmic quality of the passage, accentuated by verses that build upon each other thematically, has steered many scholars to suggest that Paul has adapted here for his purposes an early Christian song or poem. While there is debate over this claim, what does seem clear is that Paul thinks of the Christ event as part of a deeper divine story playing out against a cosmic backdrop. Traditionally called the Christ Hymn, the hymn portrays the dramatic divestiture of divine status undertaken by Christ.

In a manner that recalls the opening lines of the Prologue to the Fourth Gospel, the Christ Hymn begins by affirming the preexistence of Christ as well as the equality of divine status that

Christ shares with God (Phil. 2:6).[8] In contrast to what one encounters in the Prologue to John's Gospel, however, the hymn presses beyond this affirmation of equality and focuses on the evaluative point of view displayed by the pre-existent Christ with regard to this status of equality. Instead of regarding equality with God as a prize to cling to, Christ relinquishes such status in favor of taking on a lower status: that of a human being (2:7). Moreover, the human being envisioned by the hymn is of a particular sort: a slave. The decision to represent Jesus in his human career as a slave serves to highlight the immense measure of transformation of status that is involved in the pre-existent Christ becoming human. At the time of the Roman Empire, slaves would have occupied, of course, a distinctly unprivileged social location within the highly stratified culture of ancient society.[9] To identify Jesus as a slave, therefore, is to adopt a striking, even counter-cultural metaphor that is in creative tension with the affirmation of Christ's divine status.[10] The identification functions essentially to disorient the imaginations of those who hear the hymn and prompts them to reflect on the action of one who displays this counterintuitive attitude to a privileged status.

Normally, those who possess powerful status do not humble themselves. Yet this is precisely what the hymn says Jesus did: "He humbled himself and became obedient to the point of death—even death on a cross" (Phil. 2:8). The reference to Jesus' humility recalls the use of the same term in Paul's exhortation to the community that

---

8. There continues to be debate, however, over whether the concept of preexistence is, in fact, the best way to interpret the opening lines of the hymn. Some have proposed that an allusion, instead, to the creation of the first human beings is what is at play. On this line of argument, the statement that Christ was in the form of God functions essentially as a synonym for creation in God's image (Gen. 1:26). The strength of this proposal rests in the clear focus the hymn dedicates to the human career of Christ in the subsequent verses. Nevertheless, it seems likely that some sort of concept of Christ as having a prior spiritual existence before becoming human is in view (see also 2 Cor. 8:9; Gal. 4:4). It is possible, of course, that the passage is multivalent in its meaning.

9. See Raymond E. Brown, *An Introduction to the New Testament*, Anchor Bible Reference Library (New York: Double Day, 1997), 503–4.

10. See Udo Schnelle, *Apostle Paul: His Life and Theology*, trans. M. Eugene Boring (Grand Rapids: Eerdmans, 2005), 373.

immediately precedes the hymn: "Do nothing from selfish ambition or conceit, but in humility regard others as better than yourselves" (2:3). While left largely inexplicit, Gospel traditions relating to the passion of Jesus are likely in the background of Paul's reference to the humility and obedience of Jesus.[11] As is the case in the Gospel narratives, what seems to be of primary interest to Paul concerning the death of Jesus is not the violence inherent to the method of Jesus' execution, but the meaning of the event. The emphasis we see in the hymn on the humility and obedience of Jesus recalls the numerous stories one encounters in the Gospels that show Jesus as modeling a different way of living before God and others (see Matt. 11:28–29; Mark 9:33–37; 10:41–45; Luke 22:24–27; John 13:12–15). Ultimately it is a commitment to this kind of life that results in Jesus' death.

The hymn draws to a conclusion on a highly apocalyptic note. As a result of the exemplary quality of the human career of Jesus, God exalts or raises Jesus to new life in addition to appointing him to what appears to be a new status. The one who previously shared the status of equality with God in a state of preexistence now shares this equality in a glorified bodily existence (see Phil. 3:21). The one who was formerly a slave (2:7) is now—or at least will be—the Lord of the entire cosmos (2:10–11): "so that at the name of Jesus every knee should bend, in heaven and on earth and under the earth, and every tongue should confess that Jesus Christ is Lord, to the glory of God the Father" (2:10–11). As Paula Fredriksen observes, the "knees" envisioned at the conclusion of the hymn include heavenly or cosmic authorities in addition to human authorities.[12] Like many in the ancient world, Paul envisioned the universe as composed of multiple tiers, with each tier occupied by personalized forces. The sphere where humans resided was just one among others. The hymn therefore ends by asserting the cosmos-wide acknowledgment of the authoritative status of Christ.

The hymn leaves ambiguous the precise temporal moment at which such cosmic sovereignty is inaugurated, whether that time is

---

11. See David Wenham, *Paul: Follower of Jesus or Founder of Christianity?* (Grand Rapids: Eerdmans, 1995), 363–70.

12. Paula Fredriksen, *Paul: The Pagans' Apostle* (New Haven: Yale University Press, 2017), 139.

now, or more likely, in the future.[13] The hymn does make clear, however, that Paul considers the events referenced in the hymn to have significance for the ethical behavior of the members of the communities he wrote to. For Paul the human career of Jesus does not simply supply a behavioral model for how the faithful in the community are to live; something more radical and apocalyptic is at work in the events of the life, death, and exaltation of Jesus. As a consequence of the way Jesus lived and died, a new power has been introduced into the world according to Paul. Several times in Philippians Paul speaks to the transformative presence of this power. Confidently listing his past achievements and real privileges as an exemplary Jew, Paul sums up his attitude to these marks of honor by noting, "I want to know Christ and the power of his resurrection and the sharing of his sufferings by becoming like him in his death, if somehow I may attain the resurrection from the dead" (Phil. 3:10–11). A little later in the same chapter, Paul once more refers to the effective power of Christ's resurrection: "He will transform the body of our humiliation that it may be conformed to the body of his glory, by the power that also enables him to make all things subject to himself" (3:21). In both these passages a complex interplay is in view between the concepts of power and participation. On the one hand, Paul sees his own bodily resurrection and presumably that of the believers in Philippi as a future event. What makes Paul so confident of this future destiny, however, is the religious experience of present participation in Christ: "Not that I have already obtained this or have already reached the goal; but I press on to make it my own, because Christ Jesus has made me his own" (3:12). It is this experiential conviction that enables Paul to use highly participatory-sounding phrases such as becoming like Christ (3:10), being conformed to Christ (3:21), and having the same mind of Christ (2:5).

To have the mind of Christ is Paul's way of referring to the ethical dimension of the resurrection power that will in the future transform the very bodies of the Philippian believers. Precisely because the members of the community presently participate in Christ and therefore share in Christ's sphere of power, they are empowered to live ethically transformed lives that make it possible to attend

---

13. Fredriksen, *Paul*, 140.

radically to the interests of others (Phil. 2:4). It is this power that
flows from being found in Christ that enables Paul to view his
imprisonment (1:21; 2:17) and his past in a new way (3:7–9). The
same power is also exemplified for Paul in the form of the radically
selfless behavior of co-workers such as Timothy (2:19–22), Epaphro-
ditus (2:25–29), Euodia, Syntyche, and Clement (4:2–3). They, along
with Paul, offer the Philippian assembly personal models of what
such transformation might look like in the concrete.

The Letter to Philemon: The Occasion of the Letter

In addition to being the shortest letter by Paul preserved in the
New Testament, the Letter to Philemon represents the sole example among the uncontested correspondence of a letter written to an
individual believer rather than to an entire community.[14] Compared
to Philippians, Philemon lacks explicit references either to the death
or resurrection of Jesus. Nevertheless, the letter provides an especially
clear example of the kind of transformation in attitude and behavior
that Paul believed was made possible in the lives of believers as a
consequence of their experience of participation in Christ.

Despite the letter's brevity, the occasion that prompted Paul
to write to Philemon is surprisingly more complex than might first
appear. Philemon, in addition to being a convert, is apparently also
a slave owner (Phlm. 15–16). The social institution of slavery was
a ubiquitous reality in the urban areas of the Roman Empire, with
almost two thirds of the population occupying the status of either
slave, a child of slaves, or a former slave.[15] The social institution of
slavery in the ancient world differed in important ways from the
chattel slavery that defined eighteenth- and nineteenth-century
America. Slaves during the Roman Empire seldom endured the per-
petual lifelong slavery that accompanied the misery of forced servitude in America. Whether enslaved as a result of military captivity,

14. Nonetheless, the public character of the letter is pronounced. The letter opens,
for example, with Paul addressing other members in the house church and the letter
closes with final greetings from multiple persons who are present with Paul and who
have presumably heard Paul dictate the contents of the letter.

15. Hamm, *Philippians*, 52.

debt servitude, or simply as a result of being a child of a slave, many slaves in antiquity could look forward to freedom at some point during their adult lives. That being said, slaves had few legal rights, and it was taken for granted that they did not have personal agency over their lives or even over their own bodies. For reasons that are now unrecoverable, it appears that Philemon's slave Onesimus had sought Paul out while the latter was imprisoned, perhaps in Ephesus. It is not completely clear what, if anything, Onesimus had done to offend Philemon (18). Ambiguity also surrounds the precise nature of Paul's request to Philemon. What is clear is that Paul finds himself advocating for Onesimus as a mediator (10).

Reflections on the Rhetorical Artistry of Philemon

The Letter to Philemon offers strong evidence that although Paul was apparently not a professionally trained public speaker, he likely did have some measure of education in the craft of rhetoric, or the art of persuasive speech. Ancient authors who attended to the theory of persuasive oratory not only classified speeches according to their desired effect but attended also to the kinds of arguments that a speaker might advance to make different kinds of points.[16] Not all these arguments were of a strictly intellectual sort. Some were based on the observation taken from experience that emotions played a critical role in determining whether or not an audience could be persuaded by a given speech. Approximately half of the contents of the letter is given over to Paul's attempt to secure the good will and affection of Philemon in order to serve as a foundation for the actual request that takes up the last half of the letter.[17] To that end, Paul employs highly emotive language or what ancient rhetorical theorists called *pathos*. Twice Paul refers to the love that Philemon has displayed toward fellow believers (Phlm. 4, 7), a love that has its source in Philemon's faith in Christ (5). While Paul does not specify what these acts of love were, the impression conveyed by Paul's language is that they were tangible acts that "refreshed" or brought comfort

---

16. See the discussion in Pascuzzi, *Paul*, 61–62.

17. See Marcus Borg and John Dominic Crossan, *The First Paul: Reclaiming the Radical Visionary behind the Church's Conservative Icon* (New York: HarperOne, 2009), 36.

to fellow believers in some way (7). Philemon's faith is an embodied faith of action (6) that speaks to a community of sharing and care for others. All of this, Paul is quick to mention, fills Paul with joy and consolation as he calls to mind the kind of person Philemon has proven to be (7).

Common Life and the Transformation of Relationships

The use of *pathos* continues in verses 8–9; however, wedded to this argumentative strategy is the subtle insinuation of Paul's authoritative status in relation to Philemon, likely owing to the possible role that Paul took in converting Philemon (Phlm. 19). Earlier Paul had referred to Philemon as his brother (7), and as his friend and co-worker (1), implying a relationship of mutuality and equality, respectively. Suddenly Paul introduces more hierarchical language by signaling his prerogative to issue a command to Philemon (8). Such entitlement is apparently grounded on both Paul's status as one who has been imprisoned for his proclamation of the Gospel as well as his advanced age (9). Although Paul is quick to amend this privilege in favor of appealing to Philemon from a stance of love, the not-so-subtle point has been made. Paul's relationship with Philemon, it turns out, is defined by a complex mixture of mutuality and hierarchy that Paul uses to his own advantage (14, 21).[18]

Similar complexity appears in the letter's first reference to Onesimus. Paul turns on its head the obvious hierarchical connection he has with Onesimus in his role as mediator by designating Onesimus as both his child (Phlm. 10) and his heart (12). Paul also informs Philemon of an event that would perhaps have taken Philemon by surprise: Paul has, in a sense, given birth to a new relationship with Onesimus as a result of the latter's apparent conversion (10). Paul will eventually request of Philemon that he, too, recognize the change in relationship that now applies in his case: "Perhaps this is the reason he was separated from you for a while, so that you might have him back forever, no longer as a slave but more than a slave, a

---

18. Paul's belief that he has a special, authoritative role in relation to the communities he established comes out in a number of places in the letters (see 1 Cor. 4:15; 2 Cor. 1:2; Gal. 4:13–18).

beloved brother—especially to me but how much more to you, both in the flesh and the Lord" (15–16). Essentially, Paul wants Philemon to understand that the same relationship of mutuality that he has with his brother Paul should also characterize Philemon's relationship to his new brother, Onesimus.

While it is true that Paul stops short of repudiating the institution of slavery, this request that he makes of Philemon is at least as radical as the decision to designate Jesus as a slave in the Christ Hymn. In both cases we see deeply engrained sociological categories creatively employed to disrupt equally ingrained sensibilities. In the latter, the one who has the highest status imaginable relinquishes that status for the lowest status imaginable, while in the former Paul challenges one who has the privileged status of a master to willingly regard that status no longer as the defining mark of a particular human relationship. Implicit in all this is Paul's powerful conviction that participation in the Lord Christ is the source and ground of this new relationship (Phlm. 16). Although scholarly debate remains about what it is exactly that Paul wants Philemon to do with regard to Onesimus, there is a persuasive indication in the text that Paul wants Philemon to free Onesimus, probably in the form of early manumission:[19] "Yes, brother. Let me have this benefit from you in the Lord! Refresh my heart in Christ. Confident of your obedience, I am writing to you, knowing that you will do even more than I say" (20–21). Employing the word "love" for the third and last time in this short letter (9), Paul implies that such an embodied act of love on the part of Philemon would fit the character of one who has refreshed the hearts of the saints in the past (7).

The Letter to the Galatians: Contemporary Impressions of the Letter

It is probably the case that, for many readers, Galatians is the letter that leaves the most lasting impressions about Paul. In part this has to do with the influence Galatians has exercised in shaping the historical development of much Christian self-definition. Along with Romans, it is in Galatians where Paul singles out the response

---

19. Hamm, *Philippians*, 56.

of faith or trust as the criterion for what puts a person into a right relationship with God (see Gal. 2:15–16; 3:2, 6–14, 23–26; 5:5–6).[20] Since the time of Martin Luther and the Protestant Reformation in the fifteenth century, this perception of Paul as one who privileges faith in apparent contrast to Jewish Law observance has led many Christians to regard the concept of faith as the core religious innovation that sets apart Christianity from all other religious traditions, in particular Judaism. One of several problematic features of this appraisal, however, is the fact that Jews in Paul's day already had a lively understanding of the importance of faith. Jews trusted both that God would always remain faithful to the covenant and that one's membership in the covenant was not dependent upon earning God's approval.[21] In fact, one of the principal texts that Paul cites in support of the primacy of faith comes from the scriptures of Israel (Hab. 2:4; see Rom. 1:17; Gal. 3:11). Equally problematic is the assumption that Paul in some way minimized the importance of ethical behavior in his praise of faith. As we have seen, Paul's notion of participation in Christ actually highlights the importance that behavioral transformation played in his thinking.

Reflections on the Relationship between Faith and Torah

Since this study examines the themes of religious experience and common life, the focus of this chapter will largely be limited to these themes. It is beyond the scope of this study, for example, to address in any detailed way the complex array of issues related to the topic of how Paul regarded the status of Jewish law observance as a result of his faith commitment in Christ.[22] Some attention to this topic is warranted, however, seeing that the issue of Torah observance figures so prominently in terms of the occasion of Galatians. It is probably

---

20. Keck, *Letters*, 112–13. The English words "faith," "belief," and "believe" translate the Greek noun *pistis* and verb *pisteuō*. Both the noun and verb in Greek can connote the affective dimension of trust and loyalty as well as intellectual assent.

21. E. P. Sanders, *Paul and Palestinian Judaism: A Comparison of Patterns of Religion* (Minneapolis: Fortress, 1977), 75.

22. For a clear and accessible treatment of these issues, see Bassler, *Navigating*, 11–21.

the case that many Christians and even many non-Christians today think of Christianity and Judaism as two separate religious traditions. But this was far from the reality in Paul's day. Some twenty-five years or so after the events of Jesus' life and death, Paul could look on Gentiles who had renounced their idolatry in response to the proclamation of the gospel as persons who had become incorporated into God's covenant people, the Jewish people. Stendahl's observation on this point is apt: Paul likely would have regarded such Gentiles as having the status of being honorary Jews.[23] When one also considers that many of the Gentiles whom Paul won over to the Gospel were already sympathetic to the Jewish religion due to their familiarity with the Jewish synagogue, it is not surprising that Jewish missionaries like Paul wrestled over the question of whether Gentiles who had recently converted should live like Jews. There was even precedent for such a lifestyle. Although the instances seem to have been rare in antiquity, some Gentile males who were especially attracted to the Jewish religion took the formal step of becoming proselytes, full-fledged members of the ethnic and religious people of Israel, by having themselves circumcised. The latter entailed either the complete or partial removal of the male foreskin. It was precisely this issue—whether or not circumcision should be a requirement for Gentile males who professed faith in the Gospel—that prompted Paul to write Galatians.

While the precise circumstances that lie behind Galatians are not altogether clear, it seems that certain persons are actively encouraging the male members of the assembly to have themselves circumcised and live henceforth as proselytes guided by the legislation of Torah.[24] It is impossible to identify with any degree of certainty who these individuals were, nor even whether they were outside missionaries or members within the community itself.[25] Paul never identifies them specifically (see Gal. 1:7–9; 3:1; 4:17; 5:7, 10–12). Nor is it necessary to assume that their motivations were insincere, despite Paul's

23. Krister Stendahl, *Paul Among Jews and Gentiles* (Minneapolis: Fortress, 1976), 37.

24. See Mark Nanos, "A Jewish View," in *Four Views on the Apostle Paul*, ed. Michael F. Bird (Grand Rapids: Zondervan, 2012), 180–81.

25. For the opinion that they were rival missionaries, see Martinus C. de Boer, *Galatians: A Commentary*, New Testament Library (Louisville: Westminster John Knox, 2011), 10.

consistent efforts to discredit them (1:6–9; 6:12–13). Indeed, like Paul they probably professed a belief in Jesus as the Jewish Messiah. Unlike Paul, however, they seem to have been of the opinion that faith in the gospel proclamation was but a first step. Full maturity or perfection, understood as incorporation into the people of God, demanded as well the ritual act of circumcision, a ritual action that by Paul's time was understood by most Jews as a mark of membership among the people of Israel.[26] The high degree of anger displayed by Paul in Galatians makes it all but certain that at least some of the Galatian converts were convinced by the arguments of what we might call these rival missionaries. As converts from paganism, the members of the Galatian churches would have been accustomed to associating the realm of religiosity with matters of performance, such as prayer, ritual, and sacrifice.[27] In such a setting, an argument that advocated the necessity for a ritual action such as circumcision would likely have sounded persuasive to these Galatian converts.

Religious Experience, Common Life, and the Law of Christ

Paul arrives at his convictions on the relationship between faith and law observance less on abstract theological grounds than on the implications of his own religious experience, an experience that he assumes the Galatians likewise share: "You foolish Galatians! Who has bewitched you? It was before your eyes that Jesus Christ was publicly exhibited as crucified! The only thing I want to learn from you is this: Did you receive the Spirit by doing the works of the law or by believing what you heard? Are you so foolish? Having started with the Spirit, are you now ending with the flesh? Did you experience so much for nothing?—if it really was for nothing" (Gal. 3:1–4). It is revealing that the first argument that Paul puts forward for establishing the primacy of faith is an argument based from experience. Paul urges the Galatians to recall their original conversion

---

26. The scriptural mandate for circumcision appears in Gen. 17:9–14.

27. Thomas H. Tobin, SJ, *The Spirituality of Paul* (Eugene, OR: Wipf & Stock, 1987), 101.

experience when they trustingly accepted the proclamation concerning the death of Jesus and, as a consequence of their faith, received the Spirit. Moreover, as Paul will make clear later in this chapter and the next, the Spirit is none other than the presence of the resurrected Christ that fills and animates the collective hearts of the members of the community right now (4:6). The key to understanding why Paul begins his defense of faith in Galatians with an argument from experience lies once more in appreciating the highly participatory categories of Paul's thinking. Paul makes a point of saying that it is none other than Christ who lives in him (2:20) and that the community of the faithful have been "clothed" with Christ (3:27). And it is this participation in Christ that ultimately defines their common life as one of adoption by God (4:4–7). This participatory aspect of Paul's theological reflection is what ultimately accounts for the contrast that Paul makes in Galatians between faith and law observance (2:16–21). As Tobin notes, Paul evaluates Torah observance from a certain perspective, namely that of his own personal experience of being transformed through faith.[28] For Paul the essential substance of faith is the experiential conviction of living in Christ.

Just as he does in Philippians, Paul in Galatians draws a lesson about common life from this idea of participation in Christ. Paul would have the Galatians see that since they already have the Spirit of the resurrected Jesus living within them, they are empowered to live in a new way:

> Live by the Spirit, I say, and do not gratify the desires of the flesh. . . . But if you are led by the Spirit, you are not subject to the law. Now the works of the flesh are obvious: fornication, impurity, licentiousness, idolatry, sorcery, enmities, strife, jealousy, anger, quarrels, dissensions, factions, envy, drunkenness, carousing, and things like these. I am warning you, as I warned you before: those who do such things will not inherit the kingdom of God. (Gal. 5:16–21)

It is clear from this passage that Paul expected the Galatians to live in a manner that did not conform to the values of the surrounding

---

28. Tobin, *Spirituality*, 89.

Greco-Roman culture. Paul sharpens this counter-cultural invitation by drawing a contrast between the guidance of the Spirit, on the one hand, and the "desires of the flesh," on the other. It is important to recognize that Paul's purpose in employing this contrast is neither to diminish the physical body nor critique the expression of sexuality, which is itself a part of embodied existence. Paul uses the term "flesh" primarily to indicate self-centered behaviors that destroy community and betray love of neighbor (Gal. 5:19–21). This helps to explain why the majority of the vices that Paul includes in this list actually have little to do with sexual behavior. Paul's deeper concern, both here and in his other letters, is with the task of embodying a new way of living. The corresponding virtues that Paul proceeds to list as the "fruit" of the Sprit (5:22–23) are precisely the kinds of attitudes and behavior that cultivate common life and guard against communal dysfunctionality. And the fact that Paul can describe this life that is guided by the Sprit as the law of Christ (6:2) shows that while nothing else for Paul compares to his overwhelming experience of participation in Christ, this latter experience is what paradoxically empowers one to live the life of righteousness that, as a Jew, Paul believed was inscribed in Torah.[29]

Summary

Paul was a practical theologian whose theological reflections were motivated by his commitment to the task of shaping the communal identity of the assemblies that he had personally founded. Far from focusing on salvation as a distant, future reality, Paul more frequently spoke of salvation as a present experience of participation in Christ. While the future dimension of such participation would include the perfection of a resurrected body, even now the believer might live out of this future through the transformation of a renewed ethical life in community with others. Whether reflecting on his own imprisonment, the relationship between a master and a slave, or the relationship between faith and Torah observance, Paul consistently applied this lived experience of participation in Christ to the varied occasions envisioned in his letters.

---

29. See Bassler, *Navigating*, 20.

Questions for Review

1. How might the audience for Paul's Letter to the Philippians have reacted to the identification of Jesus as a slave in the Christ Hymn?

2. What specific episodes from the Gospels seem to be alluded to in the Christ Hymn?

3. Why is the concept of participation in Christ such an important theme in the Letter to the Philippians?

4. How does Paul's Letter to Philemon challenge deeply ingrained commitments to hierarchal models of social relationships?

5. What role does Torah play for understanding the occasion of the Letter to the Galatians?

Questions for Reflection

1. Christianity is popularly understood as a religion based on belief. Does Paul's understanding of salvation as participation in Christ support or challenge this characterization?

2. What aspects of Paul's reflections on common life might be of benefit in thinking about issues of fellowship today?

3. In what ways is Paul's thinking similar to the concepts of religious experience and common life that emerge in an analysis of the Gospels? In what ways is it different?

4. How might Paul's thoughts on issues of religious experience and common life be brought to bear on contemporary discussions of interreligious dialogue?

For Further Reading

Bassler, Jouette M. *Navigating Paul: An Introduction to Key Theological Concepts.* Louisville: Westminster John Knox, 2007.

Borg, Marcus, and John Dominic Crossan. *The First Paul: Reclaiming the Radical Visionary behind the Church's Conservative Icon.* New York: Harper One, 2009.

Brown, Raymond E. *An Introduction to the New Testament.* Anchor Bible Reference Library. New York: Doubleday, 1997.

Cousar, Charles B. *Philippians and Philemon*. The New Testament Library. Lousiville: Westminster John Knox, 2009.

de Boer, Martinus C. *Galatians: A Commentary*. New Testament Library. Louisville: Westminster John Knox, 2011.

Dunn, James D. G. *The Theology of Paul the Apostle*. Grand Rapids: Eerdmans, 1998.

Fredriksen, Paula. *Paul: The Pagans' Apostle*. New Haven: Yale University Press, 2017.

Gorman, Michael. *Apostle of the Crucified Lord: A Theological Introduction to Paul and His Letters*. Grand Rapids: Eerdmans, 2002.

Gundry, Stanley M., and Michael F. Bird. *Four Views on the Apostle Paul*. 2nd ed. Grand Rapids: Zondervan, 2012.

Hamm, Dennis, SJ. *Philippians, Colossians, Philemon*. Catholic Commentary on Sacred Scriptures. Grand Rapids: Baker 2013.

Keck, Leander. *Paul and His Letters*. Edited by Gerhard Krodel. 2nd ed. Proclamation Commentaries Series. Philadelphia: Fortress, 1988.

Nanos, Mark D. "A Jewish View." In *Four Views on the Apostle Paul*, edited by Michael F. Bird, 159–93. Grand Rapids: Zondervan, 2012.

Pascuzzi, Maria. *Paul: Windows on His Thought and World*. Winona, MN: Anselm Academic, 2014.

Sanders, E. P. *Paul and Palestinian Judaism: A Comparison of Patterns of Religion*. Minneapolis: Fortress, 1977.

Schnelle, Udo. *Apostle Paul: His Life and Theology*. Translated by M. Eugene Boring. Grand Rapids: Eerdmans, 2005.

Segal, Alan. *Paul the Convert: The Apostolate and Apostasy of Saul the Pharisee*. New Haven: Yale University Press, 1990.

Stendahl, Krister. *Paul among Jews and Gentiles*. Minneapolis: Fortress, 1976.

Tatum, Gregory, OP. *New Chapters in the Life of Paul: The Relative Chronology of His Career*. Catholic Biblical Quarterly Monograph Series 41. Washington, DC: Catholic Biblical Association, 2006.

Tobin, Thomas H., SJ. *The Spirituality of Paul.* Eugene, OR: Wipf & Stock, 1987.

Wenham, David. *Paul: Follower of Jesus or Founder of Christianity.* Grand Rapids: Eerdmans, 1995.

8

Common Life in Crisis

Paul's Response in Letters to the
Corinthians and Romans

Slightly more than halfway through 1 Corinthians, Paul introduces the image of the human body to serve as a metaphor for
thinking about the quality of common life that should define
the Corinthian community:

> Indeed, the body does not consist of one member but of
> many. If the foot would say, "Because I am not a hand, I do
> not belong to the body," that would not make it any less a
> part of the body. And if the ear would say, "Because I am
> not an eye, I do not belong to the body," that would not
> make it any less a part of the body. If the whole body were
> an eye, where would the hearing be? If the whole body were
> hearing, where would the sense of smell be? But as it is,
> God arranged the members in the body, each one of them,
> as he chose. If all were a single member, where would the
> body be? As it is, there are many members, yet one body.
> The eye cannot say to the hand, "I have no need of you," nor
> again the head to the feet, "I have no need of you. . . ." But
> God has so arranged the body, giving the greater honor to
> the inferior member, that there may be no dissension within
> the body, but the members may have the same care for one
> another." (1 Cor. 12:14–25)

Paul was not being wholly creative in his adoption of the body metaphor to discourage dissension within the community. Already by the time of Paul the body metaphor was something of a philosophical and political commonplace for conceptualizing corporate life.[1] Paul's creativity lies in the emphases he draws from the metaphor. Although it might seem as if the idea of communal unity is the primary message Paul is going for, his real contention is that diversity cultivates health in the communal setting. Moreover, it becomes clear throughout the somewhat comical conversation that ensues between the different parts of the body that diversity should not devolve into single member rule, but instead should be further enhanced through a kind of intentional privileging of those parts of the body that either are or seem to be less prominent. This latter emphasis is particularly counter-cultural in the sense that it deliberately rebels against the tendency found in most social collectives to devalue others who are deemed different and weaker for whatever reason.

It is noteworthy that Paul nowhere makes any kind of discursive argument to support the way he applies the body metaphor. Rather, Paul's reasoning lies in his experiential understanding of what it means in terms of concrete behavior to be incorporated into the dramatic story of the death and resurrection of Jesus. As Paul sees things, that event should transform every aspect of life, including interpersonal relationships. But as the Corinthian correspondence plainly shows, the task was neither an easy nor even necessarily a desirable one for many in the community.

The Conflicted Occasion behind 1 Corinthians

One of the notable features of the letters of Paul addressed thus far is the warm and affectionate tone that infuses these texts overall, with the exception of Galatians. Letters such as 1 Thessalonians, Philippians, and even a brief letter like Philemon all provide glimpses of the intense social bonds that linked Paul to the communities that he had founded. The following passage taken from 1 Thessalonians illustrates something of the depth of these social ties: "As for us, brothers

---

1. Maria Pascuzzi, *Paul: Windows on His Thought and World* (Winona, MN: Anselm Academic, 2014), 175–76.

and sisters, when, for a short time, we were made orphans by being separated from you—in person, not in heart—we longed with great eagerness to see you face to face. . . . For what is our hope, or joy or crown of boasting before our Lord Jesus at his coming? Is it not you? Yes, you are our glory and joy!" (1 Thess. 2:17–20).[2] These sentiments stand in sharp contrast to the contents of 1 and 2 Corinthians, collectively known as the Corinthian correspondence. Both letters give evidence of considerable levels of conflict over a variety of issues between Paul and certain groups within the Corinthian assembly (see esp. 1 Cor. 3:1–4; 4:8; 5:1–2; 11:16–22; 15:12; 16:10–11; 2 Cor. 2:1–4; 3:1; 6:11; 7:2–4; 10:1–13:3).[3] These conflicts elicit from Paul declarations of confusion (1 Cor. 15:12–13), anger (1 Cor. 5:1–2; 2 Cor. 13:10), sarcasm (1 Cor. 4:8; 2 Cor. 11:20–21), and even hurt feelings on his part (2 Cor. 2:1–4; 11:10–11). If one is looking for evidence of the messiness integral to interpersonal relationships, the Corinthian correspondence does not disappoint.

Soon after he had founded assemblies in both Philippi and Thessalonica (Acts 18:1–11), Paul also established a community in Corinth, the capital city of the Roman province of Achaia. According to the author of Acts, Paul spent nearly a year and a half in the city. Near the conclusion of this eighteen-month stay, around the year 51–52 CE or so, Paul appears before the Roman provincial governor Gallio on a charge of religious deviancy (Acts 18:12–17).[4]

---

2. Similar sounding passages appear in Philippians (1:7–8; 4:1, 15–16). The letter to Philemon might also be included here as an example (4–7), even though there is uncertainty both with regard to the geographical location of Philemon and the precise role Paul had in the conversion of Philemon.

3. Both 1 and 2 Corinthians attest to several visits to Corinth by Paul as well as a complicated history of multiple letters sent and received by Paul. In particular, there is a strong likelihood that 2 Corinthians in its present form is comprised of two or more separate letters written at different times to address different occasions and which have subsequently been joined together by a later editor or editors. See Calvin Roetzel, "2 Corinthians," in *The Blackwell Companion to the New Testament*, ed. David E. Aune (Chichester, UK; London; Malden, MA: Wiley Blackwell, 2010), 434–54. See also Frank J. Matera, *II Corinthians: A Commentary* (Louisville: Westminster John Knox, 2003), 24–32.

4. The region of Achaia under the empire held the status of a senatorial province. Based on both literary and rare inscriptional evidence, it would appear that Gallio was installed by the Roman senate with the official title of *proconsul* around the year 51 CE or so. See Joseph A Fitzmyer, SJ, *Paul and His Theology: A Brief Sketch*, 2nd ed. (New Jersey: Prentice, 1989), 7.

This inscription from Delphi, Greece, identifies the date that Gallio (ΓΑΛΛΙΩΝ, in the fourth line) served as proconsul in Achaia: 51-52 CE. Since Gallio was in office when Paul visited Corinth (Acts 18:12, 14, 17), the inscription pins down the date of Paul's visit there, offering a rare fixed point in the chronology of Paul's career.

Unpersuaded by the allegations against Paul, Gallio dismisses Paul, who then travels to Ephesus. First Corinthians was likely written from Ephesus several years after these events mentioned in Acts, although it probably was not the first letter that Paul had written to the community (see 1 Cor. 5:9).

The Nature of the Conflict at Corinth

Somewhat surprisingly, given Paul's lengthy stay in Corinth, challenges to his authority arose almost immediately upon his departure from the city. Some in the community were critical of Paul's refusal to accept patronage, opting instead to support himself by his own manual labor (1 Cor. 9:1–18); others appraised negatively the personal demeanor and speech abilities of Paul (see 2 Cor. 10:1, 9–11; 11:5–6); still others seem to have had reservations concerning Paul's overall trustworthiness (2 Cor. 12:16–17). On top of all this, Paul seems to have had to deal as well with criticisms arising from outside the community in the form of rival missionaries who are actively discrediting Paul's status as an apostle (2 Cor. 11:4–6; 12:11–12).

While multiple reasons contributed to Paul's strained relationship with the Corinthians, conflicting sensibilities over the question of what a Spirit-guided life should look like seem to have played an important role in the conflict (see 1 Cor. 2:1–5; 3:3–4; 14:1–5). Another likely factor in the conflict concerned issues relating to the social location of certain groups in the Corinthian community. With respect to the latter, early on in 1 Corinthians Paul addresses the assembly[5] in the following way: "Consider your own call, brothers and sisters: not many of you were wise by human standards, not many were powerful, not many were of noble birth" (1:26). This passage helpfully enables one to visualize the contours of the social makeup of the assemblies established by Paul. These were communities that represented a broad cross-section of the urban population, meaning that persons of varying socio-economic status shared fellowship in these assemblies.[6] And while the more socially affluent members of the Corinthian community were probably never in the majority, their higher status relative to less privileged members of the group likely afforded them a prominence that led to instances of communal tension and discord.[7] For example, Paul learns that there are divisions in the community arising from partisan preference for specific leaders over others (1:1–4:21), that the poorer members of the assembly are being treated dismissively by the more socially advantaged (11:18–22), that there are conflicts involved in the religious and cultural practices connected to pagan temple attendance,[8]

---

5. As noted previously, the Greek word often translated as "church" (*ekklēsia*) referred originally to the citizen body of a Greek city-state. The translation "assembly" is chosen in order better to highlight the communal dimension of the term Paul uses to describe his communities.

6. See Wayne A. Meeks, *The First Urban Christians: The Social World of the Apostle Paul* (New Haven: Yale University Press, 1983), 72–73.

7. See Gerd Theissen, *The Social Setting of Pauline Christianity: Essays on Corinth*, ed. and trans. with an introduction by John H. Schütz (Philadelphia: Fortress, 1982), 69–99. See also Meeks, *First Urban Christians*, 73.

8. The latter involved matters of unequal social status in the sense that the more socially privileged in the community likely received regular invitations to dine and socialize with their social peers within the setting of a pagan temple (1 Cor. 10:14–27), a common practice at the time. Meat that had previously been sacrificed to a pagan deity would be a staple of these meals. It seems that the more privileged groups in the community were able to successfully dissociate in their minds the polytheistic associations of these meals from their social significance. But the poorer members of the

and that particular spiritual gifts are being used self-servingly without any apparent regard for how such gifts should benefit the entire community (12:1–14:40).

These represent a selective sampling of the kinds of difficulties that placed the communal health of the Corinthian assembly in jeopardy and that prompted Paul to engage in multiple attempts at pastoral formation. One of the ways in which Paul responds to these challenges is to remind the community of the nature of the religious experience that lies at the source of their newfound identity as a new creation in Christ (2 Cor. 5:17). In turn, these reflections serve as the deeper theological context out of which Paul encourages the community to model among themselves a different manner of common life. Both of these aspects of Paul's response will be explored through an analysis of the problem of divisions in the community (1 Cor. 1:1–4:20). This section has been chosen in light of the particular relevance it bears for illuminating the themes of religious experience and common life that are the focus of this study.

Religious Experience and the Inversion of Power: 1 Cor. 1:1–4:21

As noted in the previous chapter, Paul frequently draws ethical implications from his personal and his community's religious experience of participation in Christ. As a consequence of this experience of indwelling in Christ, Paul is convinced that the members of his assemblies are empowered to live in a different way. Hence, Paul invites believers to become like Christ (Phil. 3:10), to be conformed to Christ (Phil. 3:21), to live in accordance with the law of Christ (Gal. 6:2), and to have the mind of Christ (Phil. 2:5). A similar emphasis on the theme of fellowship in Christ is also on display in the opening chapters of 1 Corinthians (1 Cor. 2:16; 3:16, 23); but in this letter the stakes appear much higher than they do, for example, in Philippians. Paul does not so much encourage the Corinthian assembly to strive to live out their new identity more perfectly as

---

church apparently could not. Since meat was something of a luxury item in the ancient diet, the few occasions when Gentile converts would have had the opportunity to consume such food would probably have been during public festivals in celebration of various pagan deities. See Theissen, *Social Setting*, 121–40.

much as he reprimands them for behaving in a manner that suggests they are not striving at all (see 1 Cor. 4:8).

As Paul sees it, some in the community are still living in accordance with false standards of power and status (1 Cor. 3:1–4) that contrast with true power as revealed in the death and resurrection of Jesus. Here it might be useful to make a few remarks concerning the language Paul uses in the opening chapters of this letter. In the space of just four chapters, Paul employs the Greek word *dynamis* ("power") a total of six times (1:18, 24; 2:4, 5; 4:19, 20). In addition, in three of these instances Paul explicitly draws a contrast between the divine power revealed in the cross or death of Jesus and human wisdom (1:18, 24; 2:5). The sheer frequency with which Paul employs the terms "power" and "wisdom" is not at all incidental to the problem of divisions that Paul addresses in the opening chapters of 1 Corinthians (1:10–4:20):[9]

> Now I appeal to you, brothers and sisters, by the name of our Lord Jesus Christ, that all of you be in agreement and that there be no divisions among you, but that you be united in the same mind and the same purpose. For it has been reported to me by Chloe's people that there are quarrels among you, my brothers and sisters. What I mean is that each of you says, "I belong to Paul," or "I belong to Apollos," or "I belong to Cephas," or "I belong to Christ." (1 Cor. 1:10–12)

While this passage makes it clear that the common life of the Corinthian community was marked by divisions, it does not identify the root causes of these divisions. To understand these causes it is necessary to place this passage into the larger context of 1 Corinthians 1:10–4:20. Of the several names mentioned in the report relayed to Paul, only two are emphasized to any significant degree in the remainder of the section: Paul and Apollos.[10]

---

9. In the first four chapters of 1 Corinthians, the Greek word translated as "power" (*dynamis*) occurs six times while the Greek word translated as wisdom (*sophia*) occurs fourteen times.

10. Apollos is mentioned a total of six times in this section of 1 Corinthians (1:12; 3:4, 5, 6, 22; 4:6). His name also appears at the conclusion of the letter (16:12). The name Paul appears a total of six times: 1:12, 13a,b; 3:4, 5; 3:22.

The book of Acts supplies our only information about Apollos (Acts 18:24–19:1). There he is identified as a Jew recently arrived in Ephesus from Alexandria in Egypt who already had committed himself to a belief in Jesus as the Messiah (18:28). The author of Acts does not provide any information on the circumstances surrounding how Apollos came to believe in Jesus, but he does impart to the reader an impression of a man who was especially gifted in public speaking and in the interpretation of scripture (18:24–26). Acts also records that Apollos was sent to Corinth by the community in Ephesus (18:27). Apparently well received in Corinth, Apollos proved himself to be a powerful and persuasive missionary figure (18:27–28). Although it is impossible to know how long Apollos stayed in Corinth, it probably was long enough for him to become a revered figure while Paul himself was engaged in his own missionary work in Ephesus (19:1–41).

Although there is little evidence that Paul saw Apollos as a rival (see 1 Cor. 4:1–6), it seems that certain groups in Corinth played off Apollos against Paul on the basis of a perception that Paul was an ineffectual preacher of the Gospel.[11] Paul as much as admits this personal limitation when he recalls for the community his first appearance in the city, a visit that also happened to coincide with the Corinthians coming to faith in the gospel: "When I came to you, brothers and sisters, I did not come proclaiming the mystery of God to you in lofty words or wisdom. . . . My speech and my proclamation were not with plausible words of wisdom, but with a demonstration of the Spirit and of power, so that your faith might rest not on human wisdom but on the power of God" (1 Cor. 2:1–5).

These verses help explain why Paul refers so frequently to wisdom in this section of the letter. In the culture of Mediterranean antiquity, eloquence was considered to be a male virtue, and especially among the highly educated there was the expectation that truthful or wise speech would also be persuasive. Compared to Apollos, Paul does not quite meet this expectation and, as a result, some in the community seem to be aligning themselves with Apollos and bragging about this alliance (1 Cor. 3:21). Paul strives, however, to

---

11. See Maria Pascuzzi, "Baptism Based Allegiance and the Divisions in Corinth: A Reexamination of 1 Cor 1:13–17," *Catholic Biblical Quarterly* 71, no. 4 (2009): 813–29.

turn such values on their head when he says, "Where is the debater of this age? Has not God made foolish the wisdom of the World" (1:20), and, "For Christ did not send me to baptize but to proclaim the gospel, and not with eloquent wisdom, so that the cross of Christ might not be emptied of its power" (1:17). The fact that Paul feels obliged to contrast human wisdom with divine wisdom and divine power (1:21–25; 2:6–7, 13) only attests to the intensity of the partisan rejection of Paul's message and authority; for his part, Paul ironically describes these persons as "wise," "strong," "held in honor" (4:10), and "arrogant" (4:19).

To his credit, Paul does not respond to the problem of divisions by exalting himself at the expense of Apollos. And while he does intimate to the Corinthians his sense of a certain preeminence given his position as the one who first founded the community in Corinth, Paul is careful to describe both Apollos and himself as equal caregivers for the community whose ultimate source, Paul insists, lies in God. Paul articulates his understanding of the status of both Apollos and himself with the aid of an agricultural metaphor: "What then is Apollos? What is Paul? Servants through whom you came to believe, as the Lord assigned to each. I planted, Apollos watered, but God gave the growth" (1 Cor. 3:5–6). This reference to the divine ground of the Corinthian common life provides an important clue to the overall pastoral strategy of Paul in these chapters. Although there are, to be sure, important sociological dimensions to the problem of the divisions at Corinth, Paul analyzes the problem of partisanship less from a sociological angle than from a narrative, theological perspective: "Has not God made foolish the wisdom of the world? For since, in the wisdom of God, the world did not know God through wisdom, God decided, through the foolishness of our proclamation, to save those who believe" (1:20–21).

John Dominic Crossan sees the opposition that Paul establishes between God's wisdom and human wisdom functioning as a critique against what he describes as the *normalcy of the world*.[12] The latter functions, for Crossan, as a descriptive category for designating the dominant social and political model of ancient agrarian societies in which a small group of powerful elites prosper through systematic

---

12. Marcus Borg and John Dominic Crossan, *The First Paul: Reclaiming the Radical Visionary behind the Church's Conservative Icon* (New York: HarperOne, 2009).

and often violent exploitation of less powerful groups.[13] At the time of the composition of 1 Corinthians, the obvious representative of such power would be the Roman Empire. While Crossan perhaps overstates the degree to which Paul singles out Roman imperial power for criticism, his instinct in coining this phrase is nonetheless insightful. Paul does in fact want the community in Corinth to perceive that they should be living in a manner that makes them distinctive with regard to the values of the surrounding culture. But more is at play here than simply a repudiation of the pattern of violence exemplified by Roman imperial practice. Manifesting itself through such behaviors as quarreling, jealousy (3:3–4), and boasting (3:21; 4:7), the deeper issue for Paul is essentially a matter of spirituality.

Here I employ the term spirituality to refer to the personal experience of participation in Christ and its embodiment in lived behavior, the very topic discussed in the previous chapter. In this instance the spirituality in view is one that regards the power that flows from participation in the Spirit as essentially a self-enhancing power. Certain groups in the Corinthian assembly are apparently reveling in this power, despite the fact that it results in purposeful disregard of others. Instances of such disregard appear with some frequency throughout the letter.

For example, certain members of the assembly point to their superior knowledge in an attempt to rationalize behavior that actually harms fellow members of the community (1 Cor. 8:7–13); the better off neglect to attend to the plight of the poorer members of the assembly (11:17–22); others in the assembly are overvaluing certain gifts of the Spirit and minimizing other gifts (14:1–5). When Paul therefore contrasts divine wisdom with human wisdom his larger point is neither to indict intellectual or cultural achievement, nor to repudiate the sociopolitical system of his age. What Paul is calling out is something more basic: the tendency found in most forms of human fellowship to think that gifts such as intellectual capacity, liberating knowledge, and forms of persuasive and inspired speech place the gifted on a higher footing than those without such gifts. Paul typically terms such behavior "flesh" and "fleshly" (3:1–3). These terms

---

13. Borg and Crossan, *The First Paul*, 135. See also, William Herzog II, *Prophet and Teacher: An Introduction to the Historical Jesus* (Louisville: Westminster, 2005), 43–69.

function for Paul to describe the sensibility or attitude of communal dysfunctionality. At root, in employing these terms Paul recognizes that, while people ought to love their neighbor, they more frequently act in ways that relate to self-interest alone.

Conceptualizing the problem of divisions in Corinth in this light helps explain why Paul uses the terminology of Spirit so frequently in this part of the letter:

> For what human being knows what is truly human except the human spirit that is within? So also no one comprehends what is truly God's except the Spirit of God. Now we have received not the spirit of the world, but the Spirit that is from God, so that we may understand the gifts bestowed on us by God. And we speak of these things in words not taught by human wisdom but taught by the Spirit, interpreting spiritual things to those who are spiritual. (1 Cor. 2:11–13)

What is Paul driving at by speaking in this way? On the one hand, he likely is echoing in this passage the "spirit" terminology that he knows certain groups in the community have adopted to celebrate their new-found identity in Christ (1 Cor. 1:7; 3:1; 12:13). Since they participate in Christ, it must follow that they have the privilege of being spiritual persons. But does it? It turns out that Paul is actually flattering the Corinthians, since he goes on to deny them the appellation and chide them for their immaturity: "I could not speak to you as spiritual people, but rather as people of the flesh, as infants in Christ. . . . Even now you are still not ready, for you are still of the flesh. For as long as there is jealousy and quarreling among you, are you not of the flesh, and behaving according to human inclinations" (3:1–3)? As Paul sees it, the spirituality of the Corinthians responsible for these divisions in the community is no spirituality at all, since it misunderstands the nature of the power that emanates from their life in Christ. This power has its source in the narrative of the cross, a narrative imprinted by the counter-cultural lifestyle of Jesus and the power of the resurrection that vindicated both his person and manner of life.[14]

---

14. See Herzog, *Prophet and Teacher*, 232. See also Marcus J. Borg, *Jesus: Uncovering the Life, Teachings, and Relevance of a Religious Revolutionary* (New York: Harper-One, 2006), 290–92.

Paul insists that he will not empty the cross of Christ of its power (1 Cor. 1:17). We have already seen in chapter 7 how, in the Philippians hymn, Paul understands the cross as the embodied expression of a life lived in radical obedience to God. This obedience, however, has a specific quality for Paul. It refers to the willingness of Jesus in his earthly career to divest himself of the highest status imaginable—equality with God—and to live a life of humility, that is, a life of serving others: "For you know the generous act of our Lord Jesus Christ, that though he was rich, yet for your sakes he became poor, so that by his poverty you might become rich" (2 Cor. 8:9). What makes such a life the source of power, however, is the vindication of Jesus through God's act of raising him from the dead. For Paul, this means in the first instance that the status quo, what Crossan describes as the normalcy of the world, cannot be the real measure of either authentic power or reality. For it follows that, if God brings life out of the apparent powerlessness of Jesus' death, the very understanding of power itself needs to be viewed in a totally different manner. As Paul sees it, the partisanship that presently defines the Corinthian community is nothing less than a denial of the power that should now define and guide their common life.

The Letter to the Romans: Paul's Vision of a Universal Common Life

The Letter to the Romans is Paul's most distinctive letter, insofar as it is the sole example of an uncontested letter written to a community that Paul had not personally founded (Rom. 1:10; 15:22).[15] The letter is also noteworthy for the challenge it poses to scholars who venture to give an account of the precise reasons that led Paul to write to the Roman community in the first place.[16] This challenge

---

15. The origins of Christianity in Rome are obscure. That said, the beginnings of the movement seem tied closely to the sizeable Jewish population already residing in Rome in the first century and in particular to the synagogues where Jews gathered in the city. See Peter Lampe, *From Paul to Valentinus: Christians at Rome in the First Two Centuries* (Minneapolis: Fortress, 2003), 7–16. See also, Raymond E. Brown and John P. Meier, *Antioch and Rome: New Testament Cradles of Catholic Christianity* (New Jersey: Paulist Press, 1983), 92–104.

16. For a sampling of the contested issues see Karl P. Donfried, ed. *The Romans Debate*, rev. and expanded ed. (Peabody, MA: Hendrickson, 1991), xlii–lxxii.

is made even more complex as a result of the important role that the Letter to the Romans came to exercise over the history of Christian theology, particularly during and after the events of the Protestant Reformation. Ever since then it has proven difficult to view the Letter to the Romans as anything other than Paul's most mature and most systematic statement of his theological convictions.[17]

Occasion for the Letter to the Romans

There is, however, at least one factor internal to Paul that might help explain why Paul wrote the letter that would turn out to be perhaps his final letter.[18] In the view of many scholars, one must look to the final chapters of Romans to understand Paul's motivations in writing the letter. In Romans 15:22–29 Paul shares his travel plans with the Roman community, informing them that he hopes to visit them before heading off to fresh missionary opportunities in Spain. In the meantime, Paul plans on bringing the collection he has amassed to Jerusalem before his visit to Rome, an enterprise over which he clearly has anxiety (see 15:30–31). Paul sums up his intentions: "So that by God's will I may come to you with joy and be refreshed in your company" (15:32). Luke Timothy Johnson notes that several Greek expressions found in the larger context of 15:22–32, translated in the NRSV as "sent on by you" (15:24) and "refreshed" (15:32), connote economic assistance.[19] With that in mind, one could argue that Paul's motivation for writing Romans was indeed internal to himself in the sense that he needed both to introduce himself to the Roman Christian community and give an account and defense of his

---

17. Thomas H. Tobin, SJ, *Pauls' Rhetoric in Its Contexts: The Argument of Romans* (Peabody, MA: Hendrickson, 2004), 2; see also Krister Stendahl, *Paul among Jews and Gentiles* (Minneapolis: Fortress, 1976), 1–2.

18. As previously noted, debate exists over whether Romans was in fact the last letter that Paul wrote. Since the scriptural evidence is not decisive on this issue, much depends on how one evaluates later testimonies in church writers who claim that Paul did make it to Spain. It is probably significant that the book of Acts ends with Paul under house arrest in Rome. Nothing more is said about his fate. If, as seems likely, Paul's appeal to the emperor was unsuccessful (Acts 25:11), then he likely died shortly after that appeal sometime during the reign of the Roman emperor Nero.

19. Luke Timothy Johnson, *The Writings of the New Testament: An Interpretation*, 3rd ed. (Minneapolis: Fortress, 2010), 304.

Gospel in the hope that the assembly in Rome might be inclined to aid him in this missionary travel. In the words of Jacob Jervell, "Paul is writing Romans mainly for himself."[20]

The reader may recall from the introduction found in chapter 6 of this study that Paul saw himself as one called by the God of Israel to proclaim the good news of Christ's death and resurrection to a non-Jewish audience (Gal. 1:16). Inspired by language found in the Jewish prophetic writings that envisioned a future age when God's blessing would extend beyond the people of Israel to include even Gentiles (in particular Isa. 49:1–6), Paul became convinced that the resurrection of Jesus marked the fulfillment of this vision in which Jew and Gentile would together live in covenantal fellowship as God's family.[21] While it is possible that many of Paul's Jewish contemporaries expected that the fulfillment of Isaiah's vision would one day be realized, probably just as many disputed that this universalizing vision had now come to pass in the historical events associated with the individual called Jesus of Nazareth. Many of these likely presumed that only in the far distant future, at the close of the age, would such a vision become reality. In the meantime, day-to-day life in the world went on visibly unchanged. Paul saw things differently. For him the foretold end-time had arrived (1 Cor. 10:11), though it had arrived in a manner quite unexpected: with the resurrection of a single individual, Jesus of Nazareth. Paul is confident that this event heralds the fulfillment of God's ultimate plan for all of humanity (see Rom. 11:25–32; 1 Cor. 15:20–28), a plan that will encompass victory over the universal enemy of death and the creation of an inclusive family of Jew and Gentle (Rom. 3:29–30; 11:25–32; 15:7–12; 1 Cor. 15:23–28). In the short interval of time remaining before the end, Paul urges the community of believers living in Rome to embody a common life that anticipates in the present the eventual fulfillment of the divine intention that Jew and Gentile live together as one in all their diversity.

---

20. Jacob Jervell, "The Letter to Jerusalem," in *Romans Debate*, ed. Donfried, 53–64, at 64.

21. For the theme of the ingathering of the Gentiles found in the Jewish Scriptures, see also Ps. 72:10–11; Isa. 11:10; 56:7–8; 60:1–7; Zech. 8:20–23.

The Strong and the Weak (Rom. 14:1–15:7)

The hallmarks of this common life are perhaps most evident in that section of Romans where Paul addresses, once again, the problem of communal divisions. Unlike the problem at Corinth, however, where partisanship over specific missionary leaders was the issue, the divisions described in Romans 14:1–15:7 reflect disagreements over table fellowship, in particular, divergent attitudes regarding food.[22] The section opens in chapter 14 with Paul referring to an undisclosed group within the Roman Christian community as the "weak," a designation that Paul employs a total of three times in the section taken as a whole (14:1–2; 15:1):

> Welcome those who are weak in faith, but not for the purpose of quarreling over opinions. Some believe in eating anything, while the weak eat only vegetables. Those who eat must not despise those who abstain, and those who abstain must not pass judgment on those who eat; for God has welcomed them. (Rom. 14:1–3)

Who are "the weak" to whom Paul refers? In an effort to provide an answer to this question, it might first be useful to consider the potential source of this category. One option is that Paul himself is responsible for coining the designation. Another option is that Paul here is adopting a designation that he knows is already in use in the Roman community. Two factors favor this latter option. First, since Paul has neither founded nor even visited the Roman community it seems unlikely that he would risk potentially alienating its members by applying to them a label that might be taken as derogatory.[23] Second, throughout this section of Romans Paul repeatedly highlights what he considers to be the inappropriate behavior of judging fellow community members (Rom. 14:3–4, 10, 13). When one combines this emphasis with the evidence of the double injunction Paul makes about the need for members of the community to "welcome" (i.e., "be accepting of") one another (14:1 and 15:7), the conclusion that

---

22. See Tobin, *Paul's Rhetoric*, 404–15. See also Kevin B. McCruden, "Judgment and Life for the Lord: Occasion and Theology of Romans 14,1–15,13," *Biblica* 86, no. 2 (2005): 229–44.

23. Tobin, *Paul's Rhetoric*, 408–9.

the term "weak" is being used by a more socially dominant group to shame another group becomes more likely.

But who precisely are these "weak" individuals who are being designated as deviant in some manner? The many references to the topic of food consumption found throughout this section of the letter suggests that the "weak" were persons who were preoccupied with matters related to Jewish dietary regulations:

> I know and am persuaded in the Lord Jesus that nothing is unclean in itself; but it is unclean for anyone who thinks it unclean. If your brother or sister is being injured by what you eat, you are no longer walking in love. Do not let what you eat cause the ruin of one for whom Christ died. . . . Do not, for the sake of food, destroy the work of God. Everything is indeed clean, but it is wrong for you to make others fall by what you eat; it is good not to eat meat or drink wine or do anything that makes your brother or sister stumble. (Rom. 14:14–21)

The fact that Paul employs in this passage the technical terminology of "clean" and "unclean" presupposes that religious judgments regarding what was appropriate and not appropriate food for Jews to eat were at the crux of the divisions affecting table fellowship in the Roman community.[24] Evidently some in the community felt at liberty to view dietary regulations as an indifferent matter as a result of the freedom they now possessed based on their experience of participation in Christ. With a note of sarcasm Paul calls this group—with which he aligns himself—the "strong" (15:1).[25] Those branded by the more dominant group as "weak," however, still took their faith commitment in Christ to be intertwined in complex ways with traditional Jewish dietary restrictions. The result of such disparate viewpoints was a common life marked by mutual recriminations from both sides (14:10).

It is tempting to interpret these different stances along divergent ethnic lines and argue accordingly that the "weak" group in Rome was comprised of Jewish Christians and the "strong" by Gentile Christians. In reality, the situation was probably more complex than

24. Tobin, *Paul's Rhetoric*, 407.

25. Tobin, *Paul's Rhetoric*, 409.

that. Given that Paul himself, though a Jew, aligns himself with the "strong" (Rom. 15:1), one must allow for the possibility that there were other Jews in the community who also embraced this position. And there could well have been Gentiles in the community who ascribed to the more religiously conservative viewpoint.[26] That said, it is interesting to note what Paul writes in Romans 15:7–9: "Welcome one another, therefore, just as Christ has welcomed you, for the glory of God. For I tell you that Christ has become a servant of the circumcised on behalf of the truth of God in order that he might confirm the promises given to the patriarchs, and in order that the Gentiles might glorify God for his mercy." In this passage Paul does seem to argue along ethnic lines by referring to "the circumcised" (Jews) and to "Gentiles." His advice to both is to "welcome" one another (15:7). As if to drive home the point of the divine intention for unity in diversity among the two groups, Paul cites a medley of scripture passages that emphasize the theme of inclusion. All this leads one to wonder, was there indeed some conflict between Jewish and Gentile Christ-believers in Rome? On this very issue, it needs to be pointed out that Paul devotes three entire chapters in Romans to a discussion of how God's promises to Israel are irrevocable (9:1–11:36). Moreover, in one of these chapters Paul warns the numerically more numerous Gentiles in the community against cultivating feelings of arrogance over against Jews (11:13–24).

However one might evaluate the historical reconstruction described above, the most important thing to notice is how Paul handles the issue dividing the "strong" and the "weak." Paul's argument transcends the mere invitation to both sides to practice mutual hospitality on the grounds of their religious commitments (Rom. 14:3–6) to include a concrete plea to the "strong" to engage in a concession:

> Let us then pursue what makes for peace and mutual upbuilding. Do not, for the sake of food, destroy the work of God. Everything is indeed clean, but it is wrong for you to make others fall by what you eat; it is good not to eat meat or drink wine or do anything that makes your brother

---

26. Tobin, *Paul's Rhetoric*, 407–8.

or sister stumble. . . . We who are strong ought to put up with the failings of the weak, and not to please ourselves. Each of us must please our neighbor for the good purpose of building up the neighbor. For Christ did not please himself. (Rom. 14:19–15:3)

The advice given here by Paul is remarkably consistent with the approach he took to the problem of partisan divisions in Corinth. In essence, Paul's invitation to the "strong" is to endeavor to embody in their common life the counter-cultural dynamic that informs the narrative of the life, death, and resurrection of Jesus. Paul would have both groups in Rome understand that this narrative of a different way taken is now the way they must travel, too.

Summary

Both the Corinthian correspondence and Paul's Letter to the Romans showcase the distinctive manner in which Paul responded to problems that had a bearing upon issues of common life in these earliest Christian communities. Paul appears in these letters as a consummate shaper of communal identity, calling upon these first-century believers in Jesus to think of power, status, and above all else their relationships with others in community in new ways. As Paul sees it, if the religious experience of participation in Christ is to have any real meaning it must entail a transformation in both outlook and behavior that opens a path to renewed common life.

Questions for Review

1. In what way does Paul creatively employ the metaphor of the human body?

2. How would you describe the way Paul responds to the problem of divisions in the Corinthian community?

3. What is one very practical reason that may account for why Paul is writing the Letter to the Romans?

4. What specific issue connected to Jewish religious observances might be informing Paul's use of the categories of the "strong" and the "weak"?

Questions for Reflection

1. How is the problem of division in the Christian community in Corinth different from the problem of division in Rome? How are the problems similar?

2. How are the problems of communal divisions at Corinth and Rome analogous to problems attending common life today? How are they different?

3. In what ways might Paul's responses to the communal divisions in both Corinth and Rome be applied to problems involving divisions in Christian communities today?

For Further Reading

Borg, Marcus J. *Jesus: Uncovering the Life, Teachings, and Relevance of a Religious Revolutionary.* New York: Harper One, 2006.

Borg, Marcus J., and John Dominic Crossan. *The First Paul: Reclaiming the Radical Visionary behind the Church's Conservative Icon.* New York: Harper, 2009.

Donfried, Karl P., ed. *The Romans Debate.* Rev. and expanded ed. Peabody, MA: Hendrickson, 1991.

Fee, Gordon D. *The First Epistle to the Corinthians.* New International Commentary on the New Testament. Grand Rapids: Eerdmans, 1987.

Fitzmyer, Joseph A., SJ. *Paul and His Theology: A Brief Sketch.* 2nd ed. Upper Saddle River, NJ: Prentice Hall. 1989.

Herzog, William R., II. *Prophet and Teacher: An Introduction to the Historical Jesus.* Louisville: John Knox, 2005.

Jervel, Jacob. "The Letter to Jerusalem." In *The Romans Debate*, edited by Karl P. Donfried, rev. and expanded ed., 53–64. Peabody, MA: Hendrickson, 1991.

Johnson, Luke Timothy. *The Writings of the New Testament: An Interpretation.* 3rd ed. Minneapolis: Fortress, 2010.

Lampe, Peter. *From Paul to Valentinus: Christians at Rome in the First Two Centuries.* Minneapolis: Fortress, 2003.

Matera, Frank J. *II Corinthians: A Commentary.* Louisville: Westminster John Knox, 2003.

McCruden, Kevin B. "Judgment and Life for the Lord: Occasion and Theology of Romans 14,1–15,13." *Biblica* 86, no. 2 (2005): 229–44.

Meeks, Wayne A. *The First Urban Christians: The Social World of the Apostle Paul.* New Haven: Yale University Press, 1983.

Pascuzzi, Maria. "Baptism Based Allegiance and the Divisions in Corinth: Reexamination of 1 Cor 1:13–17." *Catholic Biblical Quarterly* 71, no. 4 (2009): 813–29.

———. *Paul: Windows on His Thought and World.* Winona, MN: Anselm Academic, 2013.

Roetzel, Calvin. "Second Corinthians." In *The Blackwell Companion to the New Testament*, edited by David E. Aune, 434–54. Chichester, UK; London; Malden, MA: Wiley Blackwell, 2010.

Stendahl, Krister. *Paul among Jews and Gentiles.* Minneapolis: Fortress, 1976.

Theissen, Gerd. *The Social Setting of Pauline Christianity: Essays on Corinth.* Philadelphia: Fortress, 1982.

Tobin, Thomas, SJ. *Paul's Rhetoric in Its Contexts: The Argument of Romans.* Peabody, MA: Hendrickson, 2004.

Index

Note: The abbreviations *cap, t, s,* and *n* that follow page numbers indicate captions, tables, sidebars, and footnotes, respectively.